Casebook for

MODERN DATABASE MANAGEMENT

FOURTH EDITION

Casebook for

MODERN DATABASE MANAGEMENT

FOURTH EDITION

DONALD A. CARPENTER
University of Nebraska at Kearney

The Benjamin/Cummings Publishing Company, Inc.
Redwood City, California • Menlo Park, California
Reading, Massachusetts • New York • Don Mills, Ontario
Wokingham, U.K. • Amsterdam • Bonn • Sydney
Singapore • Tokyo • Madrid • San Juan

Sponsoring Editor: Larry Alexander
Associate Editor: Kathy Galinac
Production Supervisor: Larry Olsen
Designer, Compositor: Richard Kharibian
Cover Designer: Terry Hight

Copyright © 1994 by The Benjamin/Cummings Publishing Company, Inc.

All rights reserved. No part of this publication may be reproduced, stored in a database or retrieval system, or transmitted in any form or by any means, electronic, mechanical, photocopying, recording, or otherwise, without the prior written permission of the publisher. Printed in the United States of America. Published simultaneously in Canada.

ISBN 0-8053-6048-4

2 3 4 5 6 7 8 9 10--CRS--98 97 96 95 94

The Benjamin/Cummings Publishing Company, Inc.
390 Bridge Parkway
Redwood City, California 94065

Preface

This casebook is intended as a supplement to *Modern Database Management*, Fourth Edition, by Fred R. McFadden and Jeffrey A. Hoffer. This casebook is in two parts. Part I contains five cases that collectively describe a reasonably thorough set of financial accounting database requirements for a typical small business, Honest Computers Unlimited. Although the subject organization is fictitious, the cases are representative of many realistic companies. Chapter 1 presents a general journal, ledger, and financial statement subsystem. Chapters 2 through 5 each add an additional subsystem. Respectively, they are inventory management, sales and accounts receivable, purchasing and accounts payable, and payroll-related functions.

Part II presents three additional cases, each adding a realistic set of database requirements to the fundamental financial accounting database requirements of typical organizations. Chapter 6 depicts a service bureau that adds the elements of billing professional time and charges and of supporting a marketing organization. Chapter 7 presents a residential home builder with requirements for job estimating and costing. Chapter 8 presents a municipal refuse disposal agency with special needs for flexible billing, budgetary accounting, and personnel management. Each of the cases represents a realistic set of requirements, even though the organizations depicted are fictional.

Chapter 1 is intended to be tutorial. It presents a set of user views, a data flow diagram, and an entity-relationship diagram. It explains the steps of creating and normalizing relations. Exercises at the end of Chapter 1 focus on implementation using standard database languages and database management software. Chapter 1 aligns with techniques specified in McFadden and Hoffer's textbook.

Chapters 2 through 5 present pertinent user views, data flow diagrams, and entity-relationship diagrams. Chapter exercises include creating and normalizing relations plus implementation-oriented activities similar to the exercises at the end of Chapter 1.

Chapters 6, 7, and 8 present pertinent user views. End-of-chapter exercises encourage students to create data flow and entity-relationship diagrams. Other exercises include creating and normalizing relations and implementing the database.

The solutions to selected exercises are contained in the *Instructor's Manual* for the textbook.

There are several strategies for assigning cases to students. The strategy used by the author in a semester senior/graduate level database course is first to assign Chapters 1 and 2 exercises to all students. Next, each student is expected to accomplish one of the follow-on cases in Chapters 3 through 5. Solutions to those cases are presented in class so that all students are exposed to the fairly complete set of financial accounting database requirements presented by Part I. Then, students are placed on three- or four-person teams and each team is assigned one of the cases contained in Part II. The teamwork culminates with a formal in-class presentation of the case.

The author wishes to thank Professors McFadden and Hoffer for the opportunity to participate in this project and for their comments for improvement. Assistance of the Benjamin/Cummings editorial staff should also be acknowledged.

Donald A. Carpenter

Contents

PART I   **Honest Computers Unlimited**   1

     CHAPTER 1   General Journal, Ledger, and Financial Statements   3

     CHAPTER 2   Inventory Management   13

     CHAPTER 3   Sales and Accounts Receivable   19

     CHAPTER 4   Purchasing and Accounts Payable   26

     CHAPTER 5   Payroll-Related Functions   33

PART II   **Team Cases**   39

     CHAPTER 6   Celestial Customer Services   41

     CHAPTER 7   Bedrock Builders, Inc.   59

     CHAPTER 8   Eastrim County Supervisors   72

PART I

Honest Computers Unlimited

CHAPTER 1 General Journal, Ledger, and Financial Statements

CHAPTER 2 Inventory Management

CHAPTER 3 Sales and Accounts Receivable

CHAPTER 4 Purchasing and Accounts Payable

CHAPTER 5 Payroll-Related Functions

Part I describes the operations of Honest Computers Unlimited, a company founded by former college classmates Mariah Salestrom and Todd Mason. As undergraduate students, Mariah and Todd had participated in an internship project with a small business. In comparing notes with other classmates who had engaged in similar projects, they discovered a common theme. Most of the subject companies were not using their personal computer systems to their fullest potential.

After graduation, Mariah and Todd created their own company that specializes in helping small businesses to get more out of their computer systems. Honest Computers Unlimited offers a variety of services such as systems analysis and design, setting up new systems, custom programming, operator training and general troubleshooting. Those were services that many local computer sales companies did not offer to their customers. In order to gain support from those computer sales companies, Mariah and Todd decided not to sell any competing computer systems.

Each of the chapters in Part I describes an evolutionary step in the design and computerization of the database for Honest Computers Unlimited. On the advice of their certified public accountant, Mariah and Todd first set up the database for their general ledger and financial statements applications, as discussed in Chapter 1.

After being in operation a few months, Honest Computers Unlimited began to acquire an inventory of supplies and replacement/upgrade components for their clients' computer systems. Chapter 2 describes the database needs for the management of that inventory.

In a short time, Honest Computers Unlimited became a very successful organization. Word of the firm's quality services spread and the business expanded considerably. The expansion necessitated enhancing their enterprise database to incorporate sales and accounts receivable functions, as Chapter 3 explains.

The expansion of the business also resulted in a need to deal with more suppliers. Purchasing and accounts payable applications were the next to be computerized. Chapter 4 discusses the database implications of those additional applications.

Honest Computers Unlimited's growth required that Mariah and Todd hire additional workers. When the number of employees reached a significant level, it became cost justifiable to computerize the database and processing of several payroll-related functions. That impact is the topic of Chapter 5.

The material in Chapter 1 is intended to be primarily tutorial in nature, laying the framework for examination of additional applications presented in subsequent chapters. Chapters 2 through 5 each presents an application that can be studied separately from the other chapters. Collectively, the five chapters in Part I present a relatively complete set of database requirements for financial accounting applications in a typical small business.

CHAPTER 1

General Journal, Ledger, and Financial Statements

INTRODUCTION

In college, Mariah Salestrom and Todd Mason had become good friends. They both majored in information systems. They found many opportunities to work together on team projects in several college classes. Through the years, they each developed an appreciation for the quality of the other one's work.

When the time came for Mariah and Todd to engage in a business internship as part of their undergraduate programs of study, they located an employer that would hire both of them as interns. Fortunately, their duties as interns enabled them to apply the knowledge and skills they had developed in information systems.

Their internship employer had Mariah and Todd accomplish a number of projects to improve the efficiency and effectiveness of the company's computerized information system. They performed an analysis of the company's needs and recommended a number of enhancements. They installed and trained users on new application software. They redesigned the company's database and created several standard queries for managers. They set up a simple local area network for file sharing among the company's several personal computers.

By the end of their internship, Mariah and Todd developed two significant and lasting impressions. First, they enjoyed and were good at the types of activities that they had performed for their internship employer. The internship experience served to validate their choice of a college major and to justify the amount of work they had put into their studies.

Second, they were shocked to discover how inadequate their internship employer's computer information system was. That company had purchased several personal computers from a reputable local computer dealer three years prior to Mariah and Todd's involvement. The hardware and operating system was adequate and had run almost without failure. However, only a minimal amount of applications software had been purchased. The computer dealer had physically set up the computers but had not done anything to optimize the system's performance. Nor had the dealer provided any operator training. It was as if the dealer was unconcerned about any potential repeat business from this customer.

When Mariah and Todd formally presented the results of their internship, a number of classmates in the audience agreed that they had encountered similar situations in their internships or in other businesses. That caused Mariah and Todd to explore the matter further. They found that a number of literature citations which indicated that the situation was common among small businesses. They confirmed that to their satisfaction by informally surveying several local small businesses, including computer dealers.

Eventually, their findings led Mariah Salestrom and Todd Mason to found their own company, Honest Computers Unlimited. Their intention was to provide those services that small businesses need in order to make better use of their computer information systems. That included activities such as systems analysis and design support, software installation and training, system optimization and troubleshooting. When necessary, Mariah and Todd were also willing to design and create custom software applications.

Quality service was to be the hallmark of Honest Computers Unlimited. In order to provide quality service Mariah and Todd realized that they would need to sell some hardware components to upgrade clients' computer systems. However, they chose not to sell entire packaged computer systems so as not to compete with local computer dealers. They hoped to develop cooperative arrangements with such companies.

Both proprietors intended to be active in all aspects of their business. When division of labor became desirable, Mariah tended to focus more on selling their services to prospective clients, as she was more talented in that area. Todd was the stronger programmer of the two, so he was the one to develop any custom software applications that might be required.

Mariah and Todd decided to computerize their own financial accounting system, adding applications as warranted by business conditions.

USER VIEWS

On the advice of its certified public accountant, the logical application for Honest Computers Unlimited to computerize first was its general journal, general ledger, and financial statements. Three reasons were given for this approach. First, the company's business volumes were not so great as to make any other of the financial accounting applications more critical. Second, all of the other financial accounting applications would tie into the general ledger. Third, the company would be asked periodically by lenders and other interested parties for up-to-date financial statements.

The logical starting point, then, was with the general journal. It was assumed that Mariah and Todd would select a database management software package with a sufficient data definition language that would allow general ledger accounts to be added, modified, and deleted as necessary. The CPA identified two user views that would be required for the general journal activities.

The first user view allows for general journal entries to be recorded. This would be an interactive process, with the system prompting the operator to enter the appropriate data. For each journal transaction, the operator would enter a transaction number, date, and a brief description or explanation. For each line of the transaction, the operator would indicate whether the line was a debit or credit, plus the account number and dollar amount. The system would require each transaction be balanced to zero before the application can advance to another screen. Figure 1-1 illustrates the general journal entry display.

The second user view identified by the CPA is a report that shows the summary of all general journal transactions in a specified period. The report can be either displayed or printed. A format for the report is shown in Figure 1-2.

The CPA advised Honest Computers Unlimited that two user views are required for general ledger activities. The first of those is a report that recaps the general journal transactions by general ledger account. That report can be either displayed or printed. For each general ledger account, the report shows the portion of each general journal transaction that affects the balance of the general ledger account. Figure 1-3 is a facsimile of that report.

The second of the general ledger user views recommended by the CPA is the general ledger trial balance. The report lists the accounts and their balances as of the date the report is run. The report can be either printed or displayed and is shown in Figure 1-4.

The CPA advised Honest Computers Unlimited that they would need two fairly standard financial

Figure 1-1
User View 1-1: General Journal Entry Display

Journal Transaction Number: <u>93-0001</u>
Transaction Date (MM-DD-YYYY): <u>08 31 1994</u>
Description or Other Reference: <u>Two office desks & chairs</u>

Line Number	Debit or Credit	Account Number	Dollar Amount	Line Number	Debit or Credit	Account Number	Dollar Amount
1	D	220	985.24	6			
2	C	101	85.24	7			
3	C	302	900.24	8			
4				9			
5				10			

Out of balance by $ 0.00.

General Journal Transactions
08-31-94 to 09-08-94

Trans. Number	Trans. Date	Description or Reference	Acct Num.	Account Name	DR/CR	Amount
93-0001	08-31	Two office desks & chairs	220	Furniture	DR	985.24
			301	Loans payable	CR	900.00
			102	Cash in bank	CR	85.24
93-0002	09-01	Stationery	815	Office supplies	DR	26.32
			102	Cash in bank	CR	26.32
93-0003	09-02	Mt. View Community Hospital	610	Service sales	CR	775.00
			102	Cash in bank	DR	775.00
93-0004	09-05	Payment on furniture loan	301	Loans payable	DR	450.00
			102	Cash in bank	CR	450.00
93-0005	09-08	Pine Valley Furniture	610	Service sales	CR	1200.00
			102	Cash in bank	DR	1000.00
			220	Furniture	DR	200.00

Figure 1-2
User View 1-2: General Journal Recap

General Ledger Account Recap
08-31-94 through 09-08-94

Account Number: 102　　　　Account Name: Cash in bank
Normal account balance: DR　　　Beginning balance: $ 328.97

General Journal Trans. #	Date	Description or Reference	DR/CR	Amount
93-0001	08-31-94	Two office desks & chairs	CR	85.24
93-0002	09-01-94	Stationery	CR	26.32
93-0003	09-02-94	Mt. View Community Hospital	DR	775.00
93-0004	09-05-94	Payment on furniture loan	CR	450.00
93-0005	09-08-94	Pine Valley Furniture	DR	1000.00

Total Debits: $ 1775.00
Total Credits: $ 561.56
Ending Balance: $ 1542.41

Figure 1-3
User View 1-3: General Ledger Account Recap

statements, an Income Statement and a Balance Sheet, as illustrated by Figure 1-5 and Figure 1-6, respectively. Each of those reports presents general ledger account names and balances, with the accounts grouped according to standard accounting practices with appropriate group headings and totals. Both reports can be either displayed or printed.

DATA FLOW AND ENTITY-RELATIONSHIP DIAGRAMS

From their college database class, Mariah and Todd remembered that data flow diagrams and entity-relationship diagrams are two important tools for visually representing aspects of a database system. Working to-

General Ledger Trial Balance
as of 10/31/94

Account Number	Account Name	Balance	DR/CR
102	Cash in bank	$2584.27	DR
110	Marketable security	5000.00	DR
150	Parts inventory	249.99	DR
180	Prepaid insurance	740.00	DR
220	Furniture	2500.24	DR
221	Depreciation–Furn.	50.00	CR
230	Office computer	5500.00	DR
231	Depreciation–Comp.	100.00	CR
301	Loans payable	1000.00	CR
370	Taxes payable	24.50	CR
410	Notes payable	2000.00	CR
510	Owner's equity–MS	4000.00	CR
520	Owner's equity–TM	4000.00	CR
570	Retained earnings	5400.00	CR
610	Service sales	9375.00	CR
620	Supplies sales	1202.00	CR
630	Parts sales	1302.19	CR
710	Cost of service sale	6000.00	DR
720	Cost of supplies sales	1000.00	DR
730	Cost of parts sales	787.87	DR
805	Advertising expense	800.00	DR
815	Office supplies	526.32	DR
820	Office rent	2000.00	DR
825	Depreciation expense	35.00	DR
830	Insurance expense	630.00	DR
910	Interest expense	100.00	DR

Total debits: $28453.69
Total credits: $28453.69
Out of balance: $ 0.00

Figure 1-4
User View 1-4: General Ledger Trial Balance

Honest Computers Unlimited
Income Statement for period ending 10-31-1994

Revenue:
Service sales	$ 9,375.00	
Supplies sales	1,202.00	
Parts sales	1,302.19	
Total Sales		$ 11,879.19

Cost of Goods Sold:
Cost of service sales	$ 6,000.00	
Cost of supplies sales	1,000.00	
Cost of parts sales	787.87	
Total Cost of Sales		7,787.87
Gross Profit		$ 4,091.32

Expenses:
Advertising	$ 800.00	
Office supplies	526.32	
Office rent	2,000.00	
Depreciation expense	35.00	
Insurance expense	630.00	
Total Expenses		$ 3,991.32
Net Income from Operations		$ 100.00
Interest expense		100.00
Net Income		$ .00

Figure 1-5
User View 1-5: Profit and Loss Statement

gether from the user views specified by the CPA (and depicted in Figures 1-1 through 1-6), they created those diagrams. The data flow diagram (see Figure 1-7) shows that data flows from several sources through the data entry process and into the database. Then, data is drawn from that database and formatted into all of the other reports.

It should be noted that each data flow line between a source or sink of data and a transform circle is represented by a user view. That is a good cross-check to ensure that the data flow diagram is complete. If user views have been identified for which there are no corresponding data flow lines, then the data flow diagram is in error. Conversely, if there are data flow lines on the diagram for which no user view has been identified, that is an indication that work still remains to collect the missing user view (s).

Honest Computers Unlimited
Balance Sheet
as of October 31, 1994

ASSETS

Current Assets:
Cash in bank		$ 2,584.27	
Marketable security		5,000.00	
Parts inventory		249.99	
Prepaid insurance		740.00	
Total Current Assets			$ 8,574.26

Fixed Assets:
Furniture	$ 2,500.24		
Less: Depreciation	50.00	$ 2,450.24	
Office computer	5,500.00		
Less: Depreciation	100.00	5,400.00	
Total Fixed Assets			7,850.24
Total Assets			$ 16,424.50

LIABILITIES AND OWNERS' EQUITY

Current Liabilities:
Loans payable	$ 1,000.00		
Taxes payable	24.50		
Total Current Liabilities			$ 1,024.50

Long-Term Liabilities
Notes payable	$ 2,000.00		
Total Long-Term Liabilities		$ 2,000.00	
Total Liabilities			$ 3,024.50

Owners' Equity
Cash contribution–M. Salestrom		$ 4,000.00	
Cash contribution–T. Mason		4,000.00	
Retained earnings		5,400.00	
Total Owners' Equity			$ 13,400.00
Total Liabilities & Equity			$ 16,424.50

Figure 1-6

User View 1-6: Balance Sheet

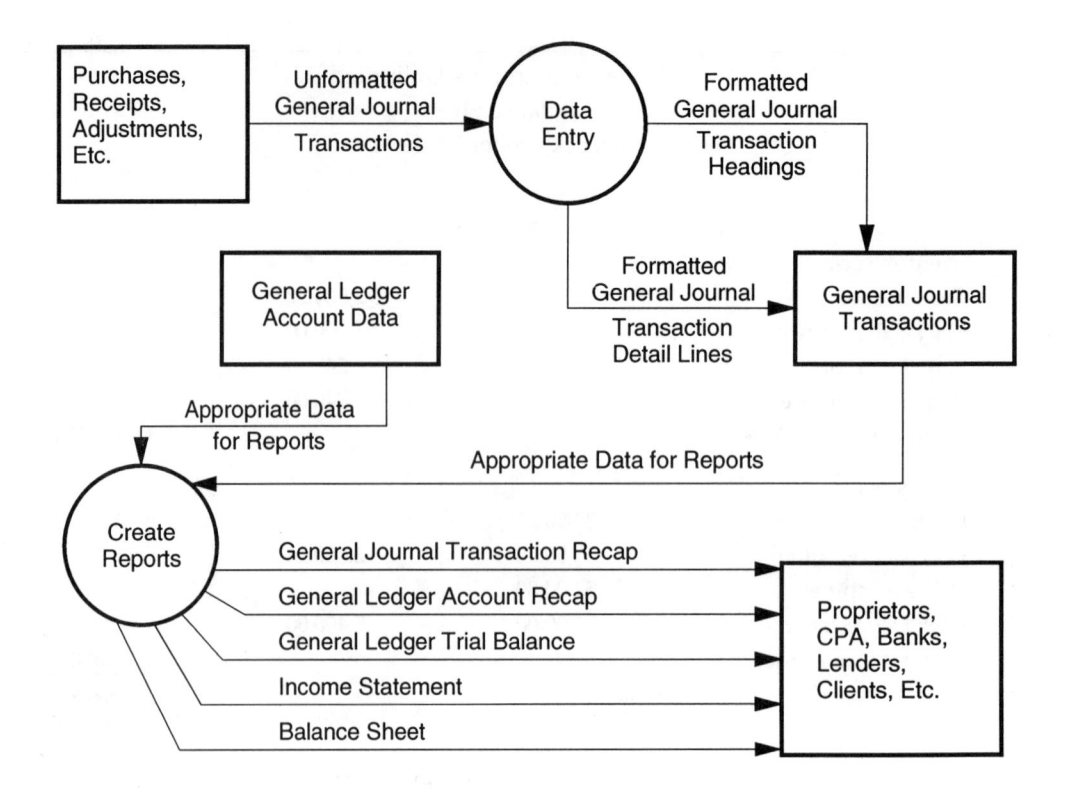

Figure 1-7

Data Flow Diagram for General Ledger, and Financial Statements

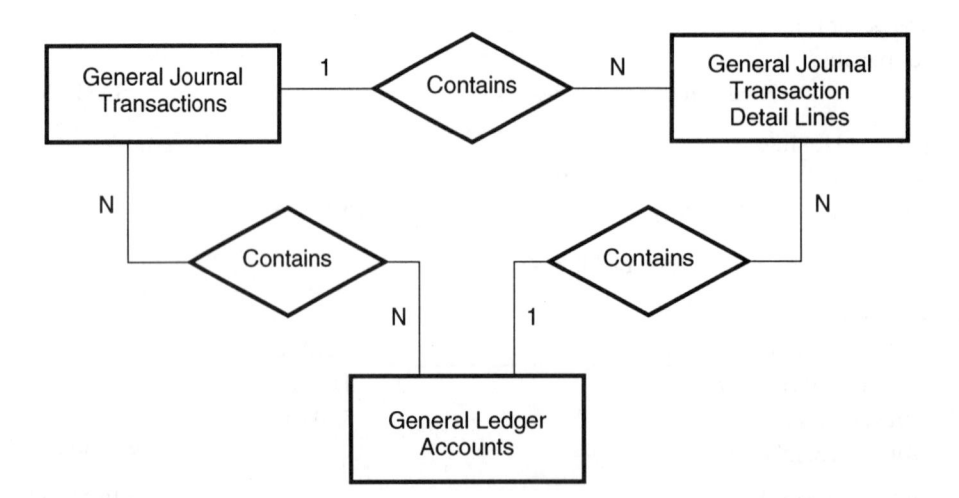

Figure 1-8

E-R Diagram for General Ledger, and Financial Statements

ENTITY-RELATIONSHIP DIAGRAMS

The entity-relationship diagram drawn by Mariah and Todd is shown in Figure 1-8. It indicates that each general journal transaction can have multiple detail lines but a given detail line can only be part of one transaction. The E-R diagram also shows that each general journal transaction detail line relates to only one general ledger account but that each general ledger account can contain several transaction detail lines. Moreover, a many-to-many relationship exists between general ledger accounts and general journal transactions.

CREATING AND NORMALIZING RELATIONS

After the user views had been identified by the CPA, Mariah and Todd could turn their attention to the processes of creating and normalizing relations. The first step is to examine each user view and to list the data elements, also known as attributes, that are required to create that user view. Headings and totals are ignored as those are added by the query or application that generates the user view.

Figure 1-9 shows the result of Mariah and Todd's efforts to create initial working relations. As there were six user views identified by the CPA, there are six groupings of data elements in the figure. No effort has yet been made to normalize these six groupings, so they are labeled as "unnormalized relations."

Strictly speaking, the groupings are not truly relations yet, as the definition of "relation" precludes the absence of any repeating groups and no examination has been made yet regarding repeating groups. Once repeating groups have been identified and eliminated, the relations can be said to be in the first normal form. So, that is the next task that faced Mariah and Todd.

Indeed, a repeating group was found in each of the three unnormalized relations that represented the general journal transaction entry display, the general journal transaction recap, and the general ledger account recap. Removal of those repeating groups resulted in the first normal form relations shown in Figure 1-10.

To move the relations to the second normal form, Mariah and Todd had to insure that all of the non-key attributes in each relation were dependent on all of the key attributes of that relation. In order to do that, they first had to identify key attributes, or unique identifiers, for each relation. In Figure 1-11, the key attributes are underlined. In three relations, two attributes are underlined indicating a concatenated key is required to uniquely identify the relation. In several instances, foreign keys appear in the relations, as indicated by the

User View 1-1
General Journal Entry Display

Journal transaction number
Transaction date
Transaction description
Line number
Debit or credit
Account number
Dollar amount

User View 1-2
General Journal Transactions Recap

Journal transaction number
Transaction date
Transaction description
Account number
Account name
Debit or credit
Dollar amount

User View 1-3
General Ledger Account Recap

Account number
Account name
Normal balance (DR or CR)
Beginning balance
Journal transaction number
Transaction date
Transaction description
Debit or credit
Dollar amount
Ending balance

User View 1-4
General Ledger Trial Balance

Account number
Account name
Account balance
Debit or credit

User View 1-5
Income Statement

Account name
Account balance

User View 1-6
Balance Sheet

Account name
Account balance

Figure 1-9
Unnormalized Relations

User View 1-1
General Journal Entry Display

(transaction)
Journal transaction number
Transaction date
Transaction description
   (transaction line, a repeating group)
Line number
Debit or credit
Account number
Dollar amount

User View 1-2
General Journal Transactions Recap

(transaction)
Journal transaction number
Transaction date
Transaction description
   (transaction line, a repeating group)
Account number
Account name
Debit or credit
Dollar amount

User View 1-3
General Ledger Account Recap

(g.l. account)
Account Number
Account Name
Normal balance (DR or CR)
Beginning balance
Ending balance
   (transaction line, a repeating group)
Journal transaction number
Transaction date
Transaction description
Debit or credit
Dollar amount

User View 1-4
General Ledger Trial Balance

(g.l. account)
Account number
Account name
Account balance
Debit or credit

User View 1-5
Income Statement

(g.l. account)
Account name
Account balance

User View 1-6
Balance Sheet

(g.l. account)
Account name
Account balance

Figure 1-10
Relations in First Normal Form (1NF)

---

broken or dotted underline. In the relation that supports the general journal transaction recap user view, an additional relation had to be created for the account name attribute, which was found not to be dependent on the key attribute of the relation that contained it previously.

The next step was to move the relations to the third normal form by eliminating any transitive dependencies. That is to say that no attribute should be dependent on the primary key of any relation except the one that houses it. Indeed, several such transitive dependencies did exist in the second normal form relations. That is because many of the relations were duplicates or near-duplicates of other relations. Consequently, those duplicates were eliminated, resulting in the group of three third normal form relations shown in Figure 1-12. An additional step was to select appropriately descriptive titles for the relations.

Mariah and Todd then estimated the volumes for each relation and determined the nature and size of each data element. Those data are also included in Figure 1-12.

User View 1-1
G.J. Entry Display

(transaction)
Journal transaction number

Transaction date
Transaction description

(transaction line, a repeating group)
Transaction number

Line number

Debit or credit
G.L. Account number
- - - - - - - - - - - -
Dollar amount

User View 1-2
G.J. Transactions Recap

(transaction)
Journal transaction number

Transaction date
Transaction description

(transaction line, a repeating group)
Transaction number

Line number

Debit or credit
G.L. Account number
- - - - - - - - - - - -
Dollar amount

(g.l. account)
G.L. Account number

Account name

User View 1-3
G.L. Account Recap

(g.l. account)
G.L. Account number

Account name
Normal balance (DR or CR)
Beginning balance
Ending balance

(transaction line, a repeating group)
Journal transaction number

Transaction line number

Transaction date
Transaction description
Debit or credit
Dollar amount
G.L. account number
- - - - - - - - - -

UserView 1-4
G.L. Trial Balance

(g.l. account)
G.L. Account number

Account name
Account balance
Debit or credit

User Views 1-5 and 1-6
Inc. Statement and Bal. Sheet

(g.l. account)
Account name
Account balance
G.L. account number

Figure 1-11

Relations in Second Normal Form (2NF)

RELATIONS/ATTRIBUTES	VOLUME TYPE	SIZE
General Journal Transaction Heading	**50 per month**	
Journal transaction number	integer	6
Transaction date	date	8
Transaction description	character	30
General Journal Transaction Detail Line	**3 per transaction (average)**	
Transaction number	integer	6
Line number	nteger	2
G.L. account number	integer	4
Debit or credit	character	2
Dollar amount	fixed 2	8
General Ledger Account	**60 accounts**	
G.L. Account number	integer	4
Account name	character	30
Normal balance (DR or CR)	character	2
Account balance	fixed 2	9

Figure 1-12
Relations in Third Normal Form (3NF)

EXERCISES

1. Create a data structure diagram for the database in this case following the format given in the textbook.
2. Using the volumes given in Figure 1-12, calculate an estimate of the size of the database.
3. Draw logical access maps (LAMs) and data base action diagrams (DADs) for each of the user views presented in the case.
4. Map the conceptual model of the database to the hierarchical, network and relational logical models.
5. Write the SQL statements necessary to implement the database and the user views shown in the case.
6. Write the QBE statements necessary to implement the database and the user views shown in the case.
7. Implement the database, add sample data and produce the user views shown in the case using an available SQL or QBE DBMS.
8. Create a data dictionary for the case.

CHAPTER 2

Inventory Management

INTRODUCTION

Honest Computers Unlimited had quite a successful beginning. Their consulting business was as good as Mariah Salestrom and Todd Mason had hoped for. They had done work for several clients, many of whom had learned of their quality services from satisfied customers. Those referrals were especially gratifying.

To their pleasant surprise, Mariah and Todd found that their sales of computer supplies and hardware replacement components had grown considerably faster than they had anticipated. There were two reasons for that.

The reason for their highly successful sales of computer supplies was their unique approach. Todd and Mariah used their supplies sales as a prospecting tool for selling their services. They carried diskettes, ribbons, and paper with them in their cars on all sales calls. That allowed them to impress prospective customers with immediate delivery of supplies. Equally impressive was their willingness to format diskettes and install ribbons and paper free of charge. They also offered substantial discounts and an unconditional guarantee on all supplies.

The reason for their unexpectedly large number of components sales to the rapidly increasing popularity of multimedia capabilities on personal computers. They found a very significant number of clients who had heard of the exciting multimedia capabilities but had no idea how to begin to install those features on their existing personal computers. The local computer sales companies offered very little help for those clients, as the typical computer sales personnel didn't know much more about upgrading to multimedia than the clients. Furthermore, the local computer companies' sales staffs made more commission on sales of new complete systems than on components. Consequently, they strongly encouraged replacing rather than upgrading existing computer systems. That provided a wide-open market for Honest Computers Unlimited to pursue.

The unexpectedly large supplies and components sales volumes also had negative aspects. So that they could provide immediate delivery, Mariah and Todd found it necessary to maintain an inventory of supplies. In order to maximize their profits by taking advantage of quantity purchase discounts, Honest Computers Unlimited also developed a significant inventory of hardware and software components.

As their inventory increased, so did Mariah and Todd's headaches. They discovered several recurring problems. First, there were times when they ran out of some inventory items because they had failed to order from their suppliers in time. Second, there were times when they had too much inventory of some items because they had each reordered without telling the other. Third, they found themselves making too many trips to the back room where they kept the inventory because they could not remember how many of a particular item were in stock. Fourth, they continually neglected to update the supplies and components inventory accounts in the general ledger to reflect the receipts of new stock from their suppliers and the issues of inventory to their clients.

Mariah and Todd decided to expand Honest Computers Unlimited's computerized enterprise database to allow them to better manage their inventory of supplies and components. Specifically, they wanted to ensure that all four of the problems listed above would be overcome.

USER VIEWS

Mariah and Todd decided that there should be a user view to reflect the inventory data entry process. This user view would be an interactive display allowing the operator to input the transactions that affect the number of units on hand and the value of the inventory items. The operator would input the inventory item number and the system would display the description of the item for verification, the current quantities on hand and on order, and the general ledger account number that would be affected. Then the operator would type in whether the transaction reflected an order that had been placed with a supplier, a receipt of a shipment of goods from the supplier, or the delivery of inventory items to a client. Next the operator would type in the number of items affected and the price per unit. Figure 2-1 shows that inventory data entry user view.

The other user views for the inventory management subsystem are reports that can be either printed or displayed. Figure 2-2 shows the first of those, which is simply a recap of all inventory transactions for an indicated period. The transactions are sorted and grouped by date. The view uses a format similar to the inventory transaction data entry display.

Figure 2-3 is a summary listing of all inventory items. It indicates the inventory item numbers and descriptions. It also shows units on hand, units on order, cost per unit, selling price per unit, and the value (at replacement cost) of the inventory items on hand. A total value of the inventory is given at the end of the report.

The next user view is somewhat of a combination of the previous two views. It is a listing of all inventory items that had activity for the given period with all the transactions that affected each item. The transactions are sorted by date. It shows the number, description, units on hand, units on order, and corresponding general ledger account number for each inventory item. It also indicates the details of each transaction for that inventory item. That view is presented as Figure 2-3.

An exception report is also required that shows any items that are at or beyond the point where an order should be placed with a supplier to replenish the stock. Figure 2-5 shows an example of that important user view.

The last user view that needs to be produced for the inventory management subsystem is a recap of the dollar figures that should be entered as general journal transactions. Also shown on this report for verification purposes are the dollar values that should be reflected in the inventory accounts in the general ledger after the postings have been made. Figure 2-6 illustrates this very important user view.

DATA FLOW AND ENTITY-RELATIONSHIP DIAGRAMS AND VOLUMES

The data flow diagram shown in Figure 2-7 is a reflection of the six user views described above and illustrated in Figures 2-1 through 2-6. The data flow diagram shows that the inventory subsystem is comprised of a data entry process that records orders placed with vendors and receipts of inventory items from those vendors as well as deliveries to clients. Those data are reflected in inventory transactions that are held in the database and then output onto several user views along with static data about the inventory items.

The entity-relationship diagram drawn by Mariah and Todd is shown in Figure 2-8. It indicates that each inventory transaction can have multiple detail lines but a given detail line can be part of only one transaction. The E-R diagram also shows that each inventory detail line relates to only one inventory item and to

INVENTORY TRANSACTIONS DATA ENTRY
November 20, 1994

INVENTORY ITEM	DESCRIPTION	QTY ON HAND	QTY ON ORDER	G/L AC #	ORD REC/ DEL	QTY	PRICE
46832	Pin Drop sound board	0	1	150	ord	2	94.99
1141	SCSI ribbon cable	2	3	150	rec	3	8.50
239876	RealPic CD/ROM drive	0	0	150	ord	1	156.00
1141	SCSI ribbon cable	5	0	150	del	1	10.50

Figure 2-1

User View 2-1: Inventory Transaction Entry Display

INVENTORY TRANSACTION RECAP
November 1, 1994 through December 1, 1994

DATE/ INVENTORY ITEM #	DESCRIPTION	G/L AC #	ORD/ REC/ DEL	QTY	PRICE
11/01/94					
6532	Epstone prntr ribbon	160	ord	24	2.50
11/05/94					
1141	SCSI ribbon cable	150	ord	1	8.50
8231	TrueFeed paper	160	rec	400	5.00
11/08/94					
8231	TrueFeed paper	160	del	50	10.00
46832	Pin Drop sound board	150	del	1	125.00
11/14/94					
1965B	key top replacements	150	rec	96	.20
11/16/94					
1141	SCSI ribbon cable	150	ord	2	8.50
1965B	key top replacements	150	del	192	1.00
11/20/94					
1141	SCSI ribbon cable	150	rec	3	8.50
1141	SCSI ribbon cable	150	del	1	10.50
46832	Pin Drop sound board	150	ord	2	94.99
23987	RealPic CD/ROM drive	150	ord	1	156.00
11/21/94					
8231	TrueFeed pape	160	del	125	9.50
8231	TrueFeed paper	160	del	80	9.75
11/24/94					
8231	TrueFeed paper	160	ord	300	5.00
11/28/94					
1141	SCSI ribbon cable	150	del	2	10.50

Figure 2-2

User View 2-2: Inventory Transaction Recap

INVENTORY SUMMARY LISTING
December 1, 1994

INVENTORY ITEM #	DESCRIPTION/DATE	HAND	QTY ON ORDER	QTY ON COST	UNIT PRICE	UNIT VALUE
1141	SCSI ribbon cable	3	0	8.50	10.50	25.50
1965B	key top replacements	7	200	.20	1.00	1.40
6532	Epstone prntr ribbon	2	24	2.50	4.00	5.00
8231	TrueFeed paper	52	300	5.00	9.50	260.00
46832	Pin Drop sound board	0	2	94.99	125.00	.00
239876	RealPic CD/ROM drive	0	1	156.00	199.99	.00

TOTAL INVENTORY VALUE AT COST = $ 291.90

Figure 2-3

User View 2-3: Inventory Summary Listing

Figure 2-4
User View 2-4: Inventory Listing with Detail Transactions

INVENTORY LISTING WITH DETAIL TRANSACTIONS
November 1, 1994 through December 1, 1994

INVENTORY ITEM #	DESCRIPTION/DATE	QTY ON HAND	QTY ON ORDER	G/L AC #	ORD/REC/DEL	QTY	PRICE
1141	SCSI ribbon cable	3	0	150			
	11/05/94				ord	1	8.50
	11/16/94				ord	2	8.50
	11/20/94				rec	3	8.50
	11/20/94				del	1	10.50
	11/28/94				del	2	10.50
1965B	key top replacements	7	200	150			
	11/14/94				rec	96	.20
	11/16/94				del	192	1.00
6532	Epstone prntr ribbon	2	24	160			
	11/01/94				ord	24	2.50
8231	TrueFeed paper	52	300	160			
	11/05/94				rec	400	5.00
	11/08/94				del	50	10.00
	11/21/94				del	125	9.50
	11/21/94				del	80	9.75
	11/24/94				ord	300	5.00
46832	Pin Drop sound board	0	2	150			
	11/08/94				del	1	125.00
	11/20/94				ord	2	94.99
239876	RealPic CD/ROM drive	0	1	150			
	11/20/94				ord	1	156.00

Figure 2-5
User View 2-5: Inventory ReOrder Listing

INVENTORY REORDER LISTING

INVENTORY ITEM #	DESCRIPTION	QTY ON HAND	QTY ON ORDER	REORDER POINT	QTY	UNIT COST
1141	SCSI ribbon cable	3	0	5	20	8.50
46832	Pin Drop sound board	0	2	0	5	94.99
239876	RealPic CD/ROM drive	0	1	0	2	156.00

GENERAL JOURNAL TRANSACTIONS FROM INVENTORY ACTIVITY
December 3, 1994

TRANS. NUMBER	TRANS. DATE	DESCRIPTION	ACCT NUM.	ACCOUNT NAME	DR/CR	AMOUNT
93-0287	12-03	Supplies Orders	161	Supply On Order	DR	236.31
			300	Accounts Payable	CR	236.31
93-0288	12-03	Supplies Received	160	Supply Inventory	DR	82.00
			161	Supply On Order	CR	82.00
93-0289	12-03	Parts Delivered	710	Cost-Part Sales	DR	147.99
			150	Parts Inventory	CR	147.99
93-0290	12-03	Supplies Received	150	Parts Inventory	DR	401.50
			151	Parts On Order	CR	401.50

Figure 2-6

User View 2-6: General Journal Transactions from Inventory

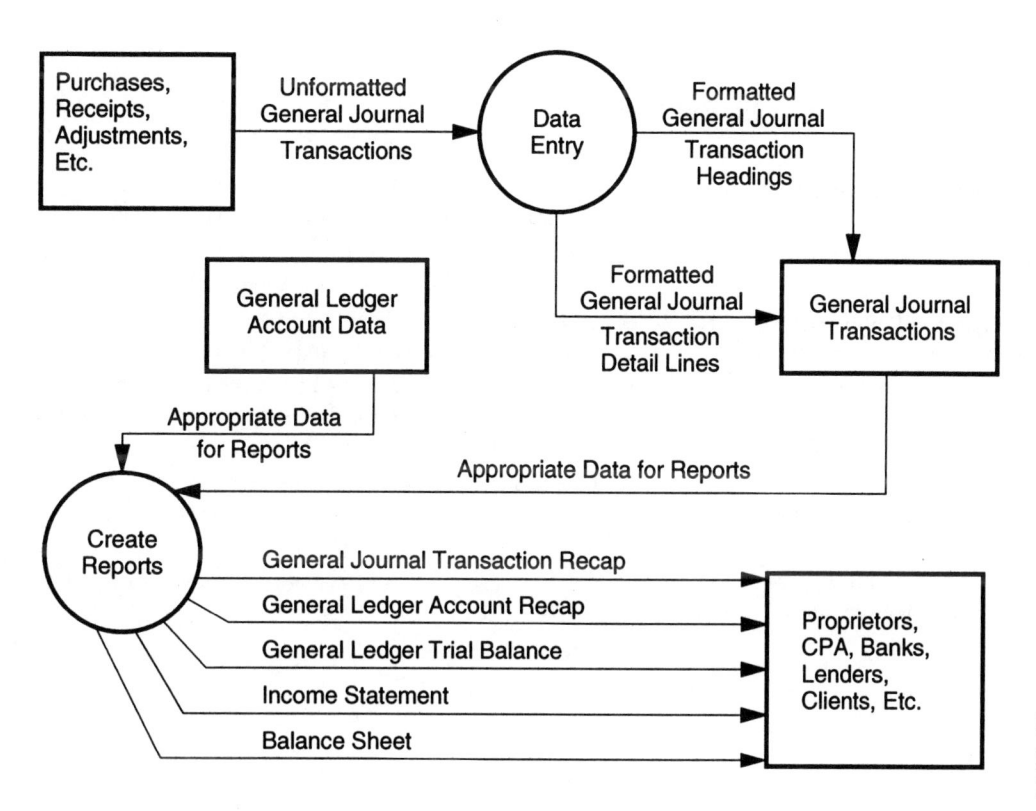

Figure 2-7

Data Flow Diagram for Inventory Management

only one general ledger account. Conversely, each inventory item and each general ledger account can contain several inventory transaction detail lines.

Mariah and Todd did some preliminary estimates of volumes of transactions. Their data indicate that there are approximately eighty inventory transactions each month and that each inventory transaction contains an average of 2.3 detail lines. They also estimated that they will ultimately carry approximately 300 distinct inventory items in stock. They determined that inventory quantities should allow for thousands of units and millions of dollars and that inventory numbers should be up to ten characters and stock descriptions should be up to twenty characters.

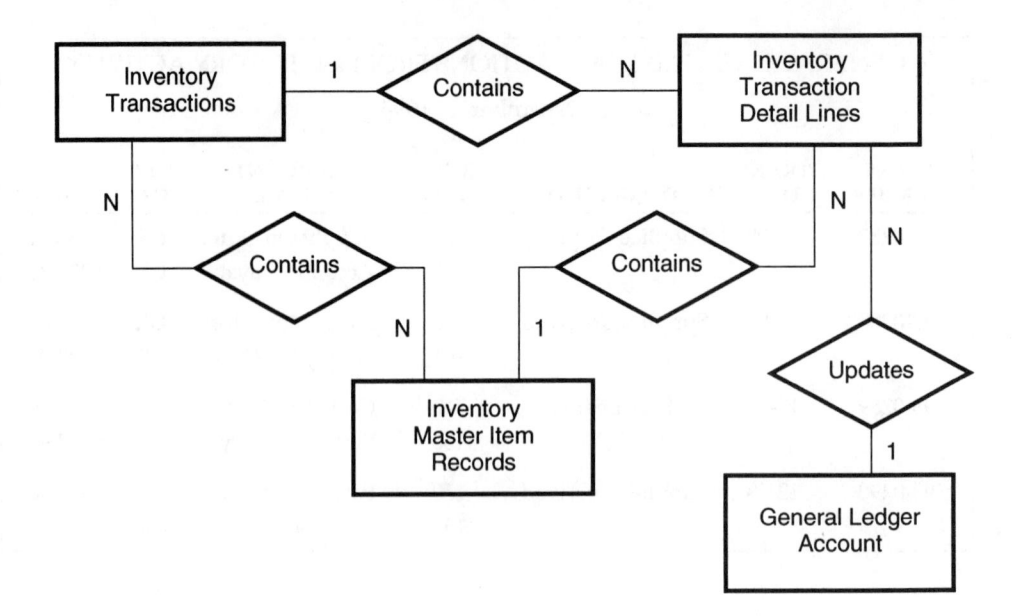

Figure 2-8
E-R Diagram for Inventory Management

EXERCISES

1. Create unnormalized relations for the database in this case.
2. Normalize the relations to at least the third normal form.
3. Integrate this set of normalized relations with the set created of normalized relations from Chapter 1. Re-normalize the integrated set of relations as may be required.
4. Create a data structure diagram for the database in this case following the format given in the text book.
5. Using the volumes given in the case, calculate an estimate of the size of the database.
6. Draw logical access maps (LAMs) and data base action diagrams (DADs) for each user view presented in the case.
7. Map the conceptual model of the database to the hierarchical, network, and relational logical models.
8. Write the SQL statements necessary to implement the database and the user views shown in the case.
9. Write the QBE statements necessary to implement the database and the user views shown in the case.
10. Implement the database, add sample data, and produce user views shown in the case using an available SQL or QBE DBMS.
11. Create a data dictionary for the case.

CHAPTER 3

Sales and Accounts Receivable

INTRODUCTION

The highly successful start-up of Honest Computers Unlimited provided a number of challenges to overcome. One of the biggest challenges arose as Mariah Salestrom and Todd Mason encountered demands for their time that they were unable to meet.

In particular, they found they did not have the time themselves to keep up with all the requests for service from their rapidly expanding clientele. Mariah and Todd did not want to compromise the personal service that was the hallmark of their company. They felt that was the main reason that their customers perceived their services to be of such high quality.

After weighing several alternates, Mariah and Todd arrived at a solution. They chose to involve some of their college classmates as subcontractors. They would farm out some of the customer requests to a select few friends who had been known to have done quality work on class assignments.

Mariah and Todd continued to be the ones with whom their clients had direct contact. Initially, any work done by subcontractors was accomplished away from the clients' businesses. Occasionally, some of the subcontractors' work brought them into direct contact with Honest Computers Unlimited's clients.

Gradually, Mariah and Todd developed more confidence in some of their subcontractors. They realized they still could maintain appropriate control as those subcontractors more frequently were in contact with clients. Their selectivity in dealing with the subcontractors paid an additional dividend. It resulted in more repeat business and more new clients, which, in turn, led to the need for more subcontractors. Business was good!

By using subcontractors, Honest Computers Unlimited had acquired the mechanism to grow to meet the demand for its quality services. That growth, however, gave rise to other challenges. Not the least of those was the need to track customer orders and to manage customer accounts. Mariah and Todd decided it was time to install customer sales and accounts receivable features into their company's database.

USER VIEWS

The first user view in the sales and accounts receivable set is a display used to input customer orders. The order is the beginning point in both the sales accounting and the accounts receivable subsystems. As shown in Figure 3-1, one order at a time is entered using the order entry display. The orders are numbered uniquely, with the order number doing triple duty as invoice number and shipping ticket number. The person who enters the order types in a customer number which the system uses to call up and display the corresponding customer name, billing address, and shipping address. If any of those data are missing or have changed, the system allows the operator to type the correct data. The operator types in a sales date and an estimated shipping or completion date. Then the system moves to the body of the order entry form, where the operator types in the number and quantity of the inventory item or consulting service being sold to the customer. The system calls up the appropriate inventory item's description and price, allowing the operator to change the price as necessary. The system extends the charge for the line and allows the operator to enter additional

Figure 3-1

User View 3-1: Customer Order/Invoice/Shipment Entry Display

```
                    CUSTOMER ORDER ENTRY DISPLAY
                          December 8, 1994

                                        ORDER NUMBER      472346
                                        CUSTOMER NUMBER:     124
                                        SALES DATE:     12/05/94
                                        DELIVERY DATE:  01/22/95

   SOLD TO:  Johnson Manufacturing    SHIP TO:  Johnson Manufacturing
             P.O. Box 498                       8438 Hilltop Road
             Wray, CO 80601                     Wray, CO 80601

                         ITEM                           UNIT
   QUANTITY    UNITS    NUMBER   ITEM DESCRIPTION       PRICE    EXTENSION
      2        hours      112    Install CD/ROM drive   20.00    $  40.00
      1        each    483267    Sunny CD/ROM kit      219.99      219.99
      2        cases     2178    gummed prntr labels    25.00       50.00

                                                   SUBTOTAL:    $ 309.99
              ( 40.00 non-taxable,  269.99 taxable @4%)   SALESTAX:   10.80
                                              INVOICE TOTAL:   $ 320.79
```

lines. After the last line, the system calculates subtotals for non-taxable and taxable items, then calculates sales tax and a total for the order.

After the last order has been entered, the system displays totals for the order entry run. Those totals then become general journal transactions and inventory transactions. The display of those totals is shown in Figure 3-2.

When customers make payments on their accounts, the payments need to be recorded. Figure 3-3 shows the user view that is used to enter customer payments. It also shows the totals that are generated at the end of the run which result in the creation of general journal transactions. When a customer makes a payment on account, the operator enters the customer number and the system displays the customer's name and the balance of the customer's account for verification. Then the operator enters the amount of the payment.

Figure 3-4 illustrates a user view that is used for two purposes. When it is displayed, it is used as a customer account query display and is typically accessed for one customer at a time. When it is printed, it is a customer statement of account and is typically printed for all customers in one run.

Occasionally, Mariah and Todd like to refer to a printed listing that shows the status of all customers. Such a user view is shown in Figure 3-5.

Unfortunately, as in most businesses, some Honest Computers Unlimited customers do not pay their bills on time or in total. Therefore, a user view is needed to show data for those clients who owe balances and the age of those balances. Such a user view is depicted in Figure 3-6.

DATA FLOW AND ENTITY-RELATIONSHIP DIAGRAMS AND VOLUMES

Figure 3-7 is the data flow diagram for the sales and accounts receivable subsystem. The diagram reflects all of the user views contained in Figures 3-1 through 3-6. It illustrates that data about sales and payments flows from customers through the data entry processes, where the date is formatted for the purpose of updating customer, sales, inventory, and general journal transaction files. Data is extracted from those files to produce order forms, invoices, shipping notices, and customer statements, which are sent to customers.

GENERAL JOURNAL TRANSACTIONS FROM SALES ACTIVITY
December 10, 1994

TRANS. NUMBER	TRANS. DATE	DESCRIPTION	ACCT NUM.	ACCOUNT NAME	DR/CR	AMOUNT
94-0832	12-10	Daily Sales	120	Accts Receivable	DR	2,900.00
			610	Service Sales	CR	2,900.00
94-0833	12-10	Daily Sales	120	Accts Receivable	DR	245.00
			620	Supply Sales	CR	245.00
94-0834	12-10	Daily Sales	120	Accts Receivable	DR	447.99
			630	Parts Sales	CR	447.99
94-0835	12-10	Daily Sales	710	Cost-Srvc Sales	DR	1,450.00
			350	Contract Payable	CR	1,450.00
94-0836	12-10	Daily Sales	720	Cost-Sply Sales	DR	130.00
			151	Supply Inventory	CR	130.00
94-0837	12-10	Daily Sales	730	Cost-Parts Sales	DR	250.00
			150	Parts Inventory	CR	250.00

INVENTORY TRANSACTIONS FROM SALES ACTIVITY
December 10, 1994

INVENTOR ITEM #	DESCRIPTION	G/L AC #	ORD	QTY	COST
46832	Pin Drop sound board	150	ord	1	125.00
6532	Epstone prntr ribbon	160	ord	20	2.50
8231	TrueFeed paper	160	ord	15	5.00
8231	TrueFeed paper	160	ord	1	5.00
46832	Pin Drop sound board	150	ord	1	125.00

Figure 3-2

User View 3-2: General Journal/Inventory Transactions from Sales

Data is also extracted in a variety of formats for management.

The entity-relationship diagram for the sales and accounts receivable subsystem is shown in Figure 3-8. The E-R diagram indicates that each customer can place several orders and that each order can have several lines. Each customer order line relates to one inventory item, but each inventory item can be expressed on several customer order lines. The diagram also shows a-one-to many relationship between customer and payments.

Mariah and Todd did some preliminary estimates of volumes of transactions. Their data indicates that the database for Honest Computers Unlimited should allow for approximately 500 clients, with 100 of those clients placing orders each month and 250 clients making payments each month. Each customer order will contain an average of 3.5 lines of items being sold.

CUSTOMER PAYMENT ON ACCOUNT DISPLAY
December 15, 1994

CUSTOMER NUMBER	CUSTOMER NAME	ACCOUNT BALANCE	AMOUNT PAID
432	Doug Stone Construction	250.00	250.00
1096	Marvin's Boats-arama	530.00	130.00
114	Chicago Ying Yang Emporium	1,850.99	1,850.99

GENERAL JOURNAL TRANSACTIONS FROM CUSTOMER RECEIPTS
December 15, 1994

TRANS. NUMBER	TRANS. DATE	DESCRIPTION	ACCT NUM.	ACCOUNT NAME	DR/CR	AMOUNT
94-0993	12-15	Daily Receipts	120	Accts Receivable	CR	2,230.99
			102	Cash in Bank	DR	2,230.99

Figure 3-3

User View 3-3: Payment on Account with General Ledger Entries

HONEST COMPUTERS UNLIMITED
STATEMENT OF CUSTOMER ACCOUNT

CUSTOMER NUMBER: 1118
STATEMENT DATE: December 18, 1994

CUSTOMER NAME: Krissian Burger Barn
BILLING ADDRESS: 147 Main Road
Yuma, WY 85943

TRANSACTION DATE	REFERENCE	CHARGES	PAYMENTS	BALANCE
11/30/94	Beginning Balance			$1,430.00
12/04/94	Payment on Account		430.00	1,000.00
12/12/94	Consulting Services	210.00		1,210.00
12/12/94	Lowtachi CD/ROM	149.99		1,359.99
12/12/94	Payment on Account		859.99	500.00

Figure 3-4

User View 3-4: Customer Statement/Account Inquiry

CUSTOMER ACCOUNT LISTING
December 20, 1994

CUSTOMER NUMBER/NAME	MONTH SALES	YTD SALES	MONTH PAYMENT	YTD PAYMNT	BALANCE
124 Johnson Manufacturing	319.99	1822.76	319.99	1822.76	0.00
432 Doug Stone Construction	.00	250.00	250.00	.00	0.00
1096 Marvin's Boats-arama	530.00	2530.00	.00	2000.00	530.00
114 Chicago Ying Yang Emp	1850.99	1850.99	.00	.00	1850.99
1118 Krissian Burger Barn	359.99	1789.99	1289.99	1289.99	500.00
5 Courtyard Kitchens	.00	800.00	.00	.00	800.00

Figure 3-5
User View 3-5: Customer Account Listing

AGED ANALYSIS OF OVERDUE ACCOUNTS
December 20, 1994

CUSTOMER ACCT/PHONE #/NAME CONTACT PERSON	ACCOUNT BALANCE	0-30 DAYS/LAST 30-60 DAYS/ OVER 60 DAYS	PAYMENT DATE/ AMOUNT
1118 307-555-9876 Krissian Burger Barn Drew Blank	500.00	.00 500.00 .00	12/12/94 859.99
5 315-555-1234 Courtyard Kitchens Dawn Smith	800.00	.00 .00 800.00	00/00/00 .00

Figure 3-6
User View 3-6: Aged Analysis of Overdue Customer Accounts

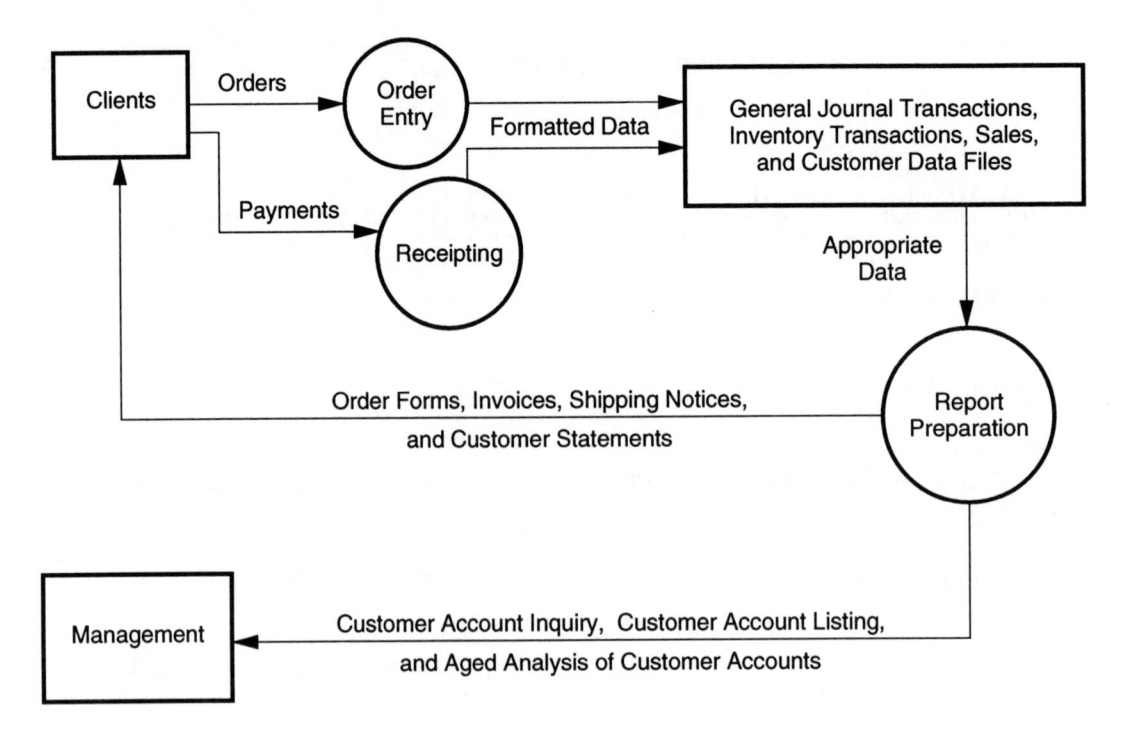

Figure 3-7
Data Flow Diagram for Sales and Accounts Receivable

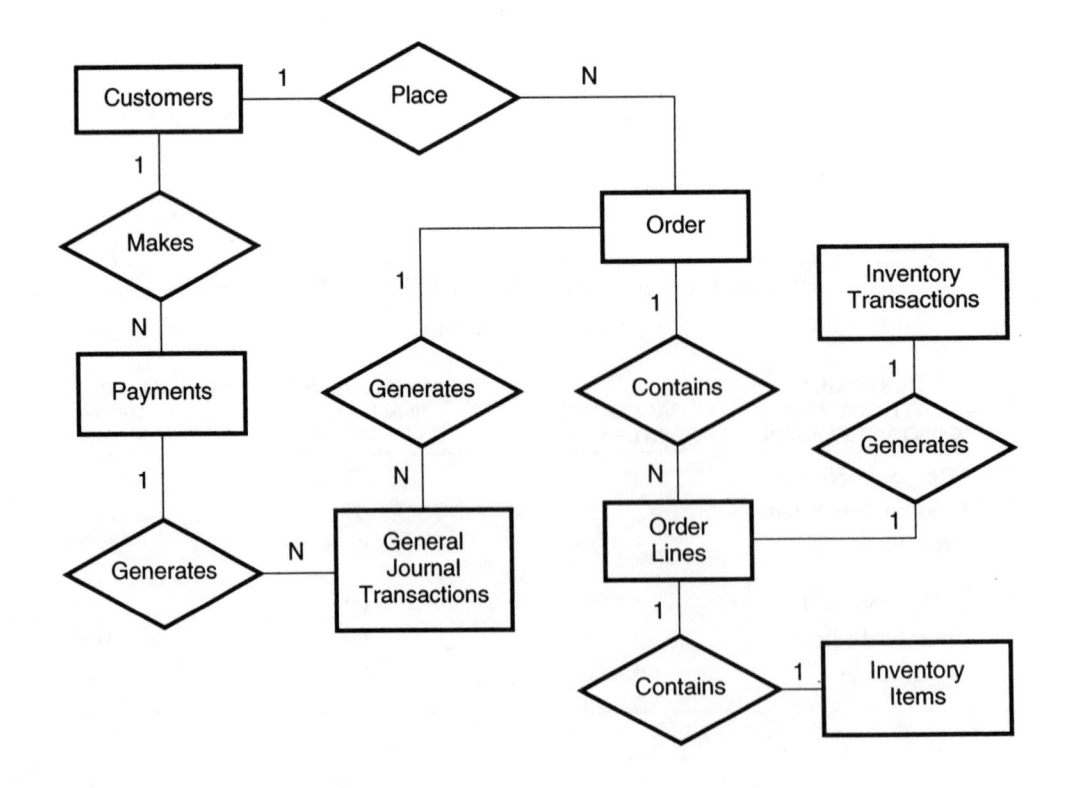

Figure 3-8
E-R Diagram for Sales and Accounts Receivable

The field sizes for customer accounts should allow for orders and balances of up to tens of thousands of dollars. Customer account numbers, order numbers and payment numbers should be up to eight numeric digits. Customer name and address fields should each be up to thirty alphanumeric characters long.

EXERCISES

1. Create unnormalized relations for the database in this case.
2. Normalize the relations to at least the third normal form.
3. Integrate this set of normalized relations with the set created of normalized relations from previous chapters. Re-normalize the integrated set of relations as may be required.
4. Create a data structure diagram for the database in this case following the format given in the textbook.
5. Using the volumes given in the case, calculate an estimate of the size of the database.
6. Draw logical access maps (LAMs) and database action diagrams (DADs) for each of user view presented in the case.
7. Map the conceptual model of the database to the hierarchical, network, and relational logical models.
8. Write the SQL statements necessary to implement the database and the user views shown in the case.
9. Write the QBE statements necessary to implement the database and the user views shown in the case
10. Implement the database, add sample data, and produce user views shown in the case using an available SQL or QBE DBMS.
11. Create a data dictionary for the case.

CHAPTER 4

Purchasing and Accounts Payable

INTRODUCTION

Mariah Salestrom and Todd Mason found that the rapid increase in Honest Computers Unlimited's sales of supplies and components parts gave rise to other challenges. For example, management of the company's inventory became a significant problem. How they met the problems of inventory management is covered in Chapter 2.

Another set of challenges brought about by increase in sales relates to dealing with the vendors that supply Honest Computers Limited with supplies and parts. There are two interrelated issues. They found the need to manage the purchasing process. They also need to manage their use of the credit accounts that vendors had established for them.

When they first established Honest Computers Unlimited, Mariah and Todd searched for the best suppliers to use. They decided that the ideal supplier would deal only in quality merchandise, would be able to respond to orders quickly with the required quantities, would be easy to deal with, and would give them a charge account. Mariah and Todd examined trade magazines, talked with local retail computer store owners, and asked purchasing managers of large organizations that used large quantities of computer supplies and component parts. They settled on vendors that met their criteria.

However, as Honest Computers Limited grew, it began to experience the same problems that typically arise in dealing with vendors. Some of their original suppliers could not keep up with the increased order volume. Other vendors raised prices. More vendors entered the market and a few left. Furthermore, as technology changed and their clientele diversified, so did the variety of products that Mariah and Todd needed to purchase.

Mariah and Todd found themselves spending much of their time locating, evaluating, and negotiating with vendors. Too much of that time was spent making lists of vendors' names, addresses, phone numbers, and their product lines and prices. They decided it was time to add that information to Honest Computers Limited's database.

Having such data in the database would also help them address the other purchasing-related problem. They were now dealing with dozens of vendors, most of whom had extended them credit. Most of the vendors expected payment within thirty days of the invoice. As Honest Computers Limited was receiving several shipments each month, including multiple shipments from some vendors each month, it had become quite a chore to track the due dates and amounts of the payments to vendors. That in turn led to difficulty in predicting the cash flow to the company. Adding vendor and purchase data to the database should help to ease that problem.

USER VIEWS

The first user view that Mariah and Todd identified was one to enter purchases placed with vendors. This user view is shown in Figure 4-1. One order at a time is entered using the order entry display and the orders are numbered uniquely. The computer operator types in a vendor number, which the system uses to call up and display the corresponding vendor name, address, and phone number. If any of those data are missing or have changed, the system allows the operator to type

```
┌─────────────────────────────────────────────────────────────────────┐
│                    PURCHASE ORDER ENTRY DISPLAY                     │
│                         JANUARY 12, 1995                            │
│                              PURCHASE ORDER NUMBER:      472346     │
│                                     VENDOR NUMBER:          124     │
│                                     PURCHASE DATE:     01/12/95     │
│                                                                     │
│   VENDOR:   Sunny Manufacturing                                     │
│             P.O. Box 498                                            │
│             Silicon Tundra, MN  50806                               │
│             (612) 555-8787                                          │
│   ─────────────────────────────────────────────────────────────     │
│                        ITEM                       UNIT              │
│   QUANTITY   UNITS    NUMBER   ITEM DESCRIPTION   PRICE  EXTENSION  │
│       1       each    483267   Sunny CD/ROM kit   129.99   129.99   │
│       2       each    483268   Sunny adaptor       14.49    28.98   │
│                                       SUBTOTAL:         $ 158.97    │
│                                      SALES TAX:            :0.80    │
│                            SHIPPING & HANDLING:             6.00    │
│                                  INVOICE TOTAL:         $ 165.77    │
└─────────────────────────────────────────────────────────────────────┘
```

Figure 4-1
User View 4-1: Purchase Order Entry Display

the correct data. The operator types in a purchase date, and the system moves to the body of the purchase order form. In the body, the operator types in the number and quantity of the inventory item being purchased. The system calls up the appropriate inventory item's description and purchase price, allowing the operator to change the price as necessary. The system extends the charge for the line and allows the operator to enter additional lines. After the last line the system calculates a subtotal and sales tax. Then it allows the operator to enter a shipping charge before it calculates the grand total for the order.

After the last order has been entered, the system displays totals for the order entry run. Those totals then become general journal transactions and inventory transactions. The display of those totals is shown in Figure 4-2.

When Honest Computers Unlimited decides to pay a vendor, the computer operator uses a display as depicted in Figure 4-3. The display looks similar to a bank check and provides the chance to edit the data before a check is printed. The operator types in the vendor number and the system displays the vendor's name and address on the check portion of the display. Then, on the remittance portion of the display, the operator types in the number of the vendor's invoice that is to be paid along with the purchase order to which the invoice relates. The dollar amount of the invoice is typed next, along with the dollar amount to be paid. The system displays the dollar amount of the corresponding purchase order. Then the operator either types more lines or requests that the system calculate and print the total on the remittance and the check portions of the display. Figure 4-3 also shows the totals that are generated at the end of the run, which result in the creation of general journal transactions.

When Mariah or Todd wants to discover which payments are due and on which dates, they can access the display that is the user view shown, Figure 4-4. The display gives a list of all payments due sorted by date. It also shows the totals by date, which serves as a cash requirements analysis.

Occasionally, Mariah and Todd like to refer to a printed listing that shows the status of all vendors, including totals for any outstanding purchase orders and unpaid invoices for each vendor. The listing also shows total purchases from each vendor for the year. Such a user view is shown in Figure 4-5.

The last user view defined by Mariah and Todd in the purchasing and accounts receivable subsystem is one that shows which vendors can supply an inventory item. It also shows the cost of the item from each vendor and the normal delivery time from each vendor. Any additional comments pertaining to quality or other considerations are also shown. That user view is depicted in Figure 4-6.

GENERAL JOURNAL TRANSACTIONS FROM PURCHASES ACTIVITY
January 15, 1995

TRANS. NUMBER	TRANS. DATE	DESCRIPTION	ACC NUM.	TACCOUNT NAME	DR/ CR	AMOUNT
95-0035	01-15	Daily Purchases	160	Parts on Order	DR	487.99
			310	Accounts Payable	CR	487.99
95-0036	01-15	Daily Purchases	161	Supply on Order	DR	145.00
			310	Accounts Payable	CR	145.00

INVENTORY TRANSACTIONS FROM PURCHASES ACTIVITY
January 16, 1995

INVENTORY ITEM #	DESCRIPTION	G/L AC #	PUR	QTY	COST
46832	Pin Drop sound board	150	pur	3	125.00
6532	Epstone prntr ribbon	160	pur	8	2.50
8231	TrueFeed paper	160	pur	20	5.00

Figure 4-2
User View 4-2: General Journal and Inventory Transactions

HONEST COMPUTERS UNLIMITED
REMITTANCE STATEMENT

VENDOR NUMBER: 124   NAME: Sunny Manufacturing   CK NO: 10076

VENDOR'S INVOICE NUMBER	INVOICE AMOUNT	OUR PURCHASE ORDER NUMBER	P.O. AMOUNT	AMOUNT PAID
8856774839	122.00	472346	164.97	122.00
8857842392	40.00	472346	164.97	40.00
8881974312	350.99	485676	225.99	200.99
			TOTAL:	62.99

CHECK NUMBER: 10076
DATE: 01/29/95

PAY TO THE ORDER OF: Sunny Manufacturing   EXACTLY: $362.99
P.O. Box 498
Silicon Tundra, MN 50806

GENERAL JOURNAL TRANSACTIONS FROM CHECK WRITING
January 29, 1995

TRANS. NUMBER	TRANS. DATE	DESCRIPTION	ACC NUM.	ACCOUNT NAME	CR	DR/ AMOUNT
95-0125	01-29	Check Writing	102	Cash in Bank	CR	884.99
			310	Accounts Payable	DR	884.99

Figure 4-3
User View 4-3: Payment Check with General Ledger Entries

ACCOUNTS PAYABLE PAYMENTS SCHEDULE
February 1, 1995 - February 10, 1995

DUE DATE	VENDOR NUMBER	VENDOR	VENDOR INVOICE	P.O. NUMBER	AMOUNT
02-03	3252	Paul's Parts Place	4456ga	387498	300.00
02-03	109	Computing Paper Inc.	11-4591	459000	247.50
02-03	2323	CDs R US	198482367	400109	82.00
02-03		SUBTOTAL DUE			629.50
02-06	109	Computing Paper Inc.	11-4672	450083	42.25
02-06		SUBTOTAL DUE			42.25
02-10	124	Sunny Manufacturing	8881974312	485676	150.00
02-10	3252	Paul's Parts Place	?	387498	1665.99
02-10	12	Acme Computer Supply	A45bf46G	399032	42.21
02-10	857	Computers Galore	?	462398	142.00
02-10		SUBTOTAL DUE			2000.20
		TOTAL DUE			2671.95

Figure 4-4

User View 4-4: List of Payments Due/Cash Requirements Analysis

VENDOR SUMMARY LISTING
February 28, 1995

VENDOR NUMBER	VENDOR NAME	INVOICES	PURCHASE ORDERS	YTD PURCHASES
8	Jim's Discount House	.00	.00	.00
12	Acme Computer Supply	.00	.00	859.99
87	Computing For Less	120.00	120.00	120.00
109	Computing Paper Inc.	335.50	643.79	643.79
124	Sunny Manufacturing	150.00	150.00	350.00
176	Sunny Retail Outlet	.00	.00	.00
857	Computers Galore	142.00	142.00	875.00
1004	Computer Parts Ltd.	.00	.00	80.00
2323	CDs R US	82.00	82.00	82.00
2879	Recycled Supplies	.00	.00	.00
3252	Paul's Parts Place	1665.99	3331.98	.00
	TOTALS	2495.49	4469.77	3010.78

Figure 4-5

User View 4-5: Vendor Summary Listing

| VENDOR OPTIONS FOR INVENTORY ITEMS |||||
| March 1, 1995 |||||
INVENTORY ITEM #	VENDOR DESCRIPTION	VENDOR NUMBER	NAME/ COMMENTS	UNIT COST
1141	SCSI ribbon cable			
		8	Jim's Discount House quick delivery	9.50
		12	Acme Computer Supply friendly	8.50
		87	Computing For Less dubious quality	8.50
1965B	key top replacements			
		1004	Computer Parts Ltd. erratic delivery	.20
6532	Epstone prntr ribbon			
		8	Jim's Discount House reliable, friendly	2.50
		12	Acme Computer Supply Todd's grandmother	2.50
		87	Computing For Less usually out of stock	1.98
		1004	Computer Parts Ltd. bait and switch	2.50
		3252	Paul's Parts Place best quality	3.35
8231	TrueFeed paper			
		109	Computing Paper Inc never out of stock	5.00
		2879	Recycled Supplies quick delivery	5.00
		3252	Paul's Parts Place often back ordered	5.00

Figure 4-6
User View 4-6: Vendor Options for Inventory Items

DATA FLOW DIAGRAM, ENTITY-RELATIONSHIP DIAGRAM, AND VOLUMES

Figure 4-7 is the data flow diagram for the purchasing and accounts payable subsystems. It includes all the aspects of those applications as reflected in the user views in Figures 4-1 through 4-6. The diagram indicates that data flows from management regarding purchase decisions and from vendors regarding their billing for purchases. Data flows into the data entry processes and is formatted and stored in the database for use in preparing purchase orders and checks for vendors, and for management reports.

The entity-relationship diagram for the purchasing and accounts payable subsystems is illustrated in Figure 4-8. It indicates a many-to-many relationship between vendor and inventory item as each vendor can supply multiple inventory items and each inventory item can be supplied by multiple vendors. It also shows that each purchase order and each check is related to only one vendor, but that a vendor can be related to multiple purchase orders and to multiple checks. Each purchase order can contain several inventory items and each inventory item can be contained on multiple purchase orders. Lastly, many-to-many relationships exist between vendor invoices and purchase orders and between vendor invoices and checks.

Chapter 4

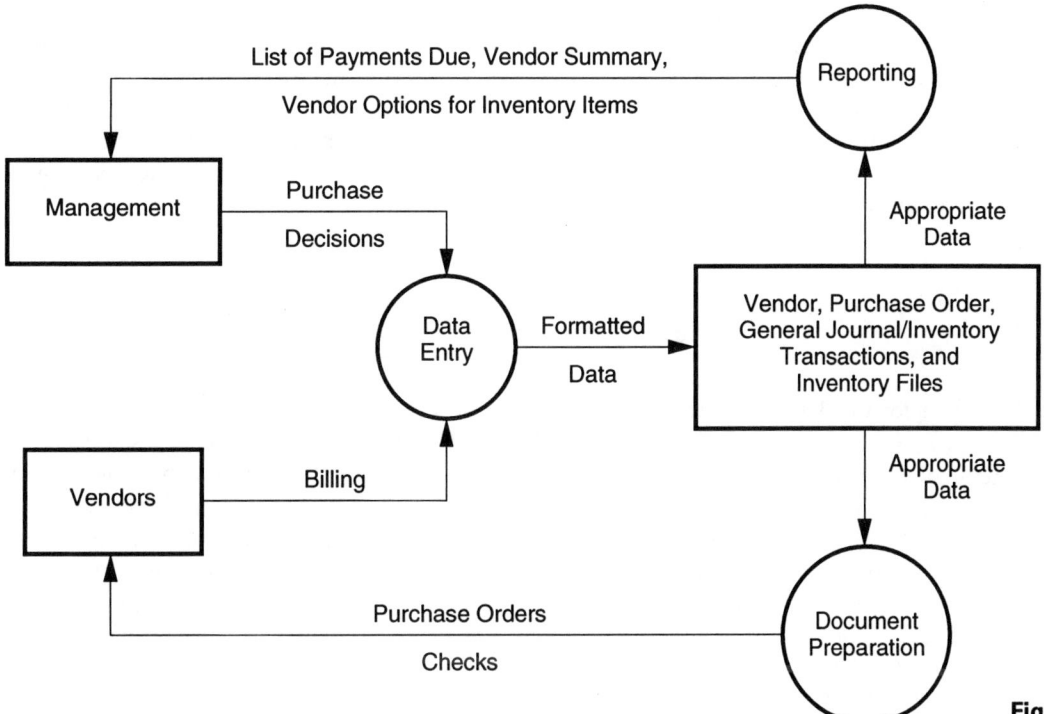

Figure 4-7
Data Flow Diagram for Sales and Accounts Receivable

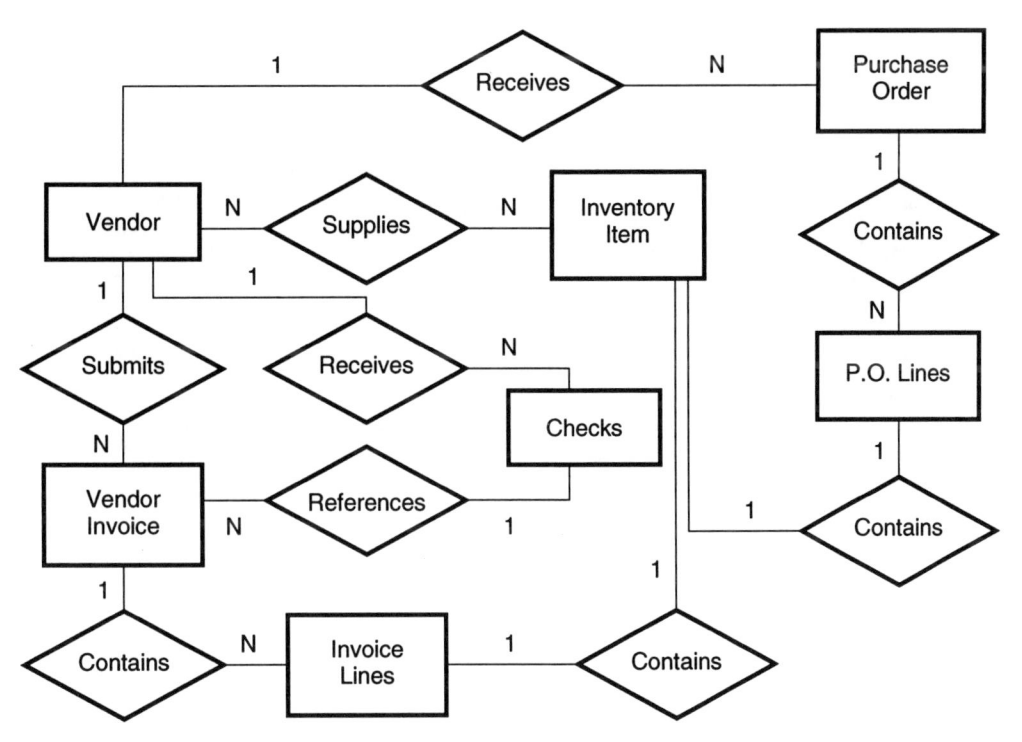

Figure 4-8
E-R Diagram for Sales and Accounts Receivable

Mariah and Todd did some preliminary estimates of volumes of transactions for the purchasing and accounts payable subsystems. Their data indicates that there are approximately two hundred vendors and three hundred inventory items. Each month there are fifty purchase orders with an average of 2.8 lines on each and thirty payments made with an average of 1.7 lines on each.

The field sizes for vendor accounts should allow for orders and balances of up to tens of thousands of dollars. Vendor account numbers, purchase order numbers, and check numbers should be up to eight numeric digits. Vendor name and address fields should each be up to thirty alphanumeric characters long, as should be vendor invoice numbers.

EXERCISES

1. Create unnormalized relations for the database in this case.
2. Normalize the relations to at least the third normal form.
3. Integrate this set of normalized relations with the set created of normalized relations from previous chapters. Re-normalize the integrated set of relations as may be required.
4. Create a data structure diagram for the database in this case following the format given in the textbook.
5. Using the volumes given in the case, calculate an estimate of the size of the database.
6. Draw logical access maps (LAMs) and data base action diagrams (DADs) for each user view presented in the case.
7. Map the conceptual model of the database to the hierarchical, network, and relational logical models.
8. Write the SQL statements necessary to implement the database and the user views shown in the case.
9. Write the QBE statements necessary to implement the database and the user views shown in the case
10. Implement the database, add sample data, and produce user views shown in the case using an available SQL or QBE DBMS.
11. Create a data dictionary for the case.

CHAPTER 5

Payroll-Related Functions

INTRODUCTION

Honest Computers Unlimited was a success. Its rapid growth was what founders Mariah Salestrom and Todd Mason had hoped for. The acceptance of their high-quality services and products was indeed gratifying. Yet, the sustained growth of their company required that Mariah and Todd spend more and more time in managing the firm and less time with customers.

As an initial solution, Honest Computers Unlimited retained services of trusted friends who performed some client-related activities on a contract basis behind the scenes. Eventually, Mariah and Todd were faced with a dilemma. Some contractors had become nearly indispensable as they knew more about the details of the work of particular clients than did Mariah and Todd. Added complications arose when some of those most valuable contractors expressed their frustration over their unsteady income levels and lack of benefits as contractors.

Mariah and Todd realized how valuable the contractors were to Honest Computers Unlimited. They also realized how financially dangerous it might be if the contractors were to open their own competing businesses or were to go to work for a competitor. Given the alternatives, Honest Computers Unlimited made offers of regular full-time salaried employment to five contractors. At the same time and on the advice of their CPA, Mariah and Todd put themselves on the payroll as salaried employees. Up to that time they had been drawing from the company earnings.

The wisdom of their decision was very quickly apparent. The contractors immediately became even more productive than they had previously been. They were allowed to locate, develop, and directly service their own clients. Mariah realized that most of her time was spent in strategy sessions and quality control meetings with the former contractors, now called consultants. In essence, Mariah became Director of Marketing for Honest Computers Unlimited.

Meanwhile, other work was consuming most of Todd's time. The decision was made to hire a secretary and two clerks. The trio handled all of the office duties and all of the internal computer operations for Honest Computers Unlimited. All three were paid an hourly wage.

Two other hourly workers were also hired to deal with the growing inventory of supplies and parts. Both worked in the warehouse area, receiving shipments, stocking shelves, and filling customer orders. Both also made deliveries to customers.

Todd became the General Manager of Honest Computers Unlimited. His primary functions were to keep the foundation of the company on solid ground. He supervised the hourly workers and negotiated with suppliers. He established and refined operational policies and procedures. He created long- and short-term plans and interfaced with the company's financial backers. Like Mariah, Todd kept a few of the longer-standing clients as his personal accounts in order to keep in touch with the original mission of Honest Computers Unlimited.

With seven salaried and five hourly employees to be paid, Mariah and Todd decided to computerize the payroll-related applications. That required the addition of several relations and attributes to the enterprise database. The following paragraphs describe the user views and conceptual diagrams around which the database would be designed for the payroll subsystem.

USER VIEWS

The first user view for the payroll subsystem is the display used to enter the time card data and to verify other data. An operator first types in the pay period ending date, then an employee's social security number, and the system displays the employee's name for verification. The system also displays the employee's hourly rate of pay or salary. If the employee is paid at an hourly rate, the operator then enters the number of regular then overtime hours. For all employees, the system allows the operator to enter additional dollars to be added to or deducted from the employee's pay. The system allows the operator to verify all data for an employee before proceeding to the next employee. This user view is depicted in Figure 5-1, which shows entered data for an hourly employee with a special deduction from net pay and entered data for a salaried employee with a special add-on to gross pay.

The next user view is the payroll check as shown in Figure 5-2. Before the payroll checks are produced, a batch program is run to calculate the gross pay, tax withholding amounts, and net pay. The payroll check has an attached statement that advises the employee as to the following data for the pay period and for the year to date: regular and overtime hours worked, pay rate (hourly or salary), other pay, gross pay, federal income tax withheld, state income tax withheld, social security (FICA) tax withheld, deduction for the employee's portion of the insurance plan, deduction for the employee's contribution to the retirement plan, deduction for U.S. Savings Bond, a miscellaneous deduction, and the net pay. The check portion of the view contains a check number, the date, the employee's name, and the dollar amount of the check.

As the payroll check writing occurs, totals for the pay period are accumulated. Figure 5-3 illustrates that several totals become part of a set of general journal transactions for the current pay period.

Figure 5-4 illustrates the employee detail data listing. It shows all the data that is on the notice attached to the paycheck for the current pay period, quarter, and year. This report can be either displayed or printed. Usually the query is performed for one employee at a time. However, the operator can choose to print the report for all employees with totals at the end.

On a quarterly basis, Honest Computers Unlimited must make its withholding tax deposits and send to the government a listing (called a 941-A report) of all employees with social security numbers and amounts of taxable wages and federal taxes withheld for the quarter. That report is shown in Figure 5-5.

After the end of the year and no later than February 1st of the next year, Honest Computers Unlimited must send W-2 statements to its employees with copies to the federal and state governments. The format of the W-2 changes quite often but Figure 5-6 captures the essence of what must be included on those statements.

DATA FLOW DIAGRAM, ENTITY-RELATIONSHIP DIAGRAM, AND VOLUMES

The data flow diagram for the payroll subsystem is shown in Figure 5-7. Data flows from the time cards into the data entry process where it is formatted and stored in the database. Data flows out of the database into the process which calculates the earnings and

Figure 5-1
User View 5-1: Payroll Time Card Entry Display

PAYROLL DATA ENTRY					
ENDING DATE	SOC SEC NUM	EMPLOYEE'S NAME			
03-10-95	506-92-9999	Frederick K. Drews			
SALARY	HOURLY RATE	REGULAR HOURS	OVERTIME HOURS	ADDITION TO GROSS	DEDUCTION FROM NET
	7.50	40.00	5.00		13.45
ENDING DATE	SOC SEC NUM	EMPLOYEE'S NAME			
03-10-95	521-21-2121	Sally Arnold-Krzywiec			
SALARY	HOURLY RATE	REGULAR HOURS	OVERTIME HOURS	ADDITION TO GROSS	DEDUCTION FROM NET
600.00				40.00	

```
                    PAYROLL CHECK ADVISORY NOTICE

    PAY PERIOD                                              SALARY OR
    ENDING DATE    SOC SEC NUM      EMPLOYEE'S NAME        HOURLY RATE

    03-10-95       506-92-9999      Frederick K. Drews      7.50/hour

                   REG.      O.T.      REG.      O.T.    ADDITION    GROSS
                   HOURS     HOURS     PAY       PAY     TO GROSS    PAY

    THIS PERIOD:   40.00     5.00      00.00     56.25     0.00      356.25
    CALENDAR YR:   120.00    15.00     900.00    168.75    12.00     1080.75

               FED    STATE   FICA    INS.    RET.    U.S.    MISC    NET
               TAX    TAX     TAX     PLAN    PLAN    BOND    DED.    PAY

    PERIOD:    52.15  21.25   22.50   10.00   .00     .00     13.45   236.90
    YEAR:      156.45 63.75   67.50   30.00   .00     .00     13.45   749.60

                                              CHECK NUMBER:      23067
                                                      DATE:      03/10/95
    PAY TO THE ORDER OF: Frederick K. Drews           EXACTLY:   $236.90
                         1234 Main Boulevard
                         Hometown, CO  80999
```

Figure 5-2

User View 5-2: Payroll Check and Advisory Notice

```
        GENERAL JOURNAL TRANSACTIONS FROM PAYROLL CHECK WRITING
                              March 10, 1995

    TRANS.    TRANS.                    ACCTA   CCOUNT           DR/
    NUMBER    DATE    DESCRIPTION       NUM.    NAME             CR    AMOUNT

    95-0421   03-10   Payroll Checks    823     Payroll Expense  DR    1845.00
                                        710     Cost-Srvc Sales  DR    5200.00
                                        102     Cash in Bank     CR    4285.00
                                        312     Taxes Withheld   CR    2185.00
                                        313     Ins. Withheld    CR    225.00
                                        314     Pension WIthheld CR    350.00
```

Figure 5-3

User View 5-3: General Journal Entries from Payroll Check Writing

taxes, then back into the database. Data then flows from the database to be formatted as pay checks to the employees and as reports to management.

The entity-relationship diagram for the payroll subsystem is very simple by comparison to some of the other subsystems. As illustrated in Figure 5-8, an employee can be paid on several payroll checks but each payroll check goes to only one employee.

Mariah and Todd did some preliminary estimates of volumes of transactions for the payroll subsystem. Their data indicates that there are twelve employees at present but that they plan to have twenty or thirty employees eventually. Employees are paid twice each month. The employee name and address information should be up to thirty alphanumeric characters for each field. Hours are floating point numbers with three digits to the left of the decimal and two digits to the right. Dollar figures for tax deductions should allow for up to tens of thousands of dollars; for other deductions, up to thousands of dollars; for all earnings fields, up to hundreds of thousands of dollars; and for the hourly rate field, up to $20 per hour.

Figure 5-4

User View 5-4: Employee Detail Listing

		EMPLOYEE DETAIL LISTING		
MOST RECENT PAY PERIOD ENDING DATE	SOC SEC NUM	EMPLOYEE'S NAME		SALARY OR HOURLY RATE
03-10-95	506-92-9999	Frederick K. Drews		7.50/hour

	REG. HOURS	O.T. HOURS	REG. PAY	O.T. PAY	ADDITION TO GROSS	GROSS PAY
THIS PERIOD:	40.00	5.00	300.00	56.25	0.00	356.25
FOR QUARTER:	120.00	15.00	900.00	168.75	12.00	1080.75
CALENDAR YR:	120.00	15.00	900.00	168.75	12.00	1080.75

	FED TAX	STATE TAX	FICA TAX	INS. PLAN	RET. PLAN	U.S. BOND	MISC DED.	NET PAY
PERIOD:	52.15	21.25	22.50	10.00	.00	.00	13.45	236.90
QTR:	156.45	63.75	67.50	30.00	.00	.00	13.45	749.60
YEAR:	156.45	63.75	67.50	30.00	.00	.00	13.45	749.60

Figure 5-5

User View 5-5: 941-A Quarterly Government Tax Report

	941-A QUARTERLY REPORT			
SOC SEC NUM	NAME	QUARTER EARNINGS	FEDERAL INC. TAX WITHHELD	FICA TAX WITHHELD
506-92-9999	Frederick K. Drews	1080.75	156.45	67.50
521-21-2121	Sally Arnold-Krzywiec	1800.00	425.65	126.60
457-35-9999	Mariah Salestrom	3000.00	859.78	210.00
635-45-111	Todd A. Mason	3000.00	859.78	210.00

Figure 5-6

User View 5-6: W-2 Year-End Wage and Tax Statement

W-2 WAGE AND TAX STATEMENT

	FEDERAL INCOME TAX WITHHELD: 156.45		WAGES, TIPS & OTHER COMPENSATION: 1080.75
EMPLOYEE SOCIAL SECURITY NUMBER: 506-92-9999	SOCIAL SECURITY TAX WITHHELD: 67.50		SOCIAL SECURITY WAGES: 1080.75
EMPLOYEE NAME & ADDRESS: Frederick K. Drews 1234 Main Boulevard Hometown, CO 80999	STATE TAX WITHHELD: 63.75	STATE: Colorado	STATE WAGES, TIPS, ETC. 1080.75

Chapter 5 **37**

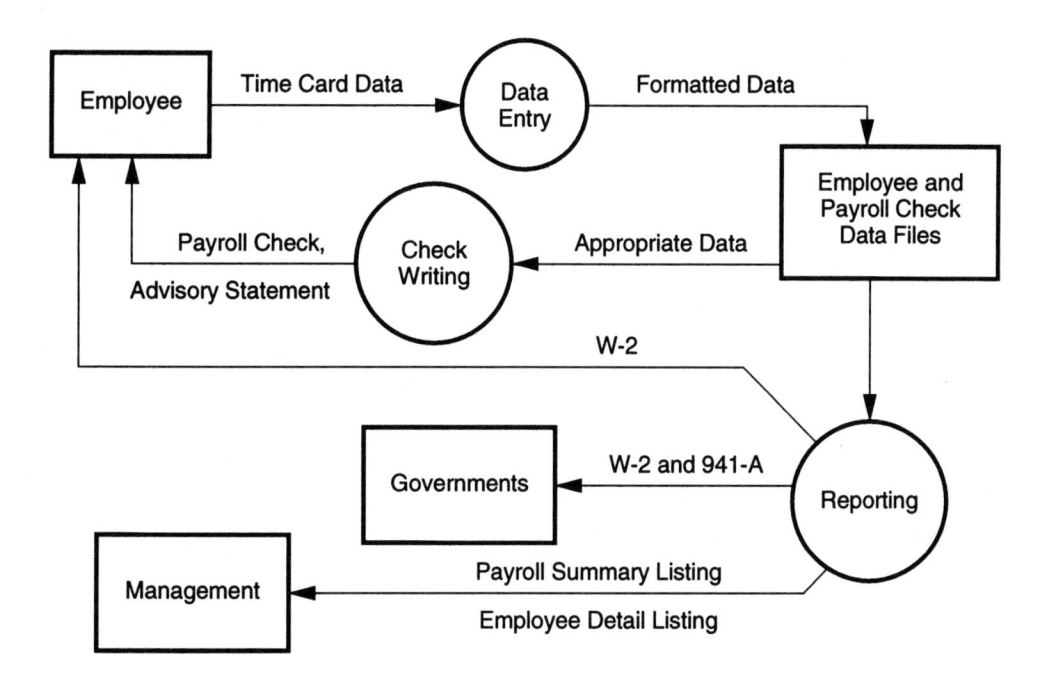

Figure 5-7
Data Flow Diagram for Payroll Related Functions

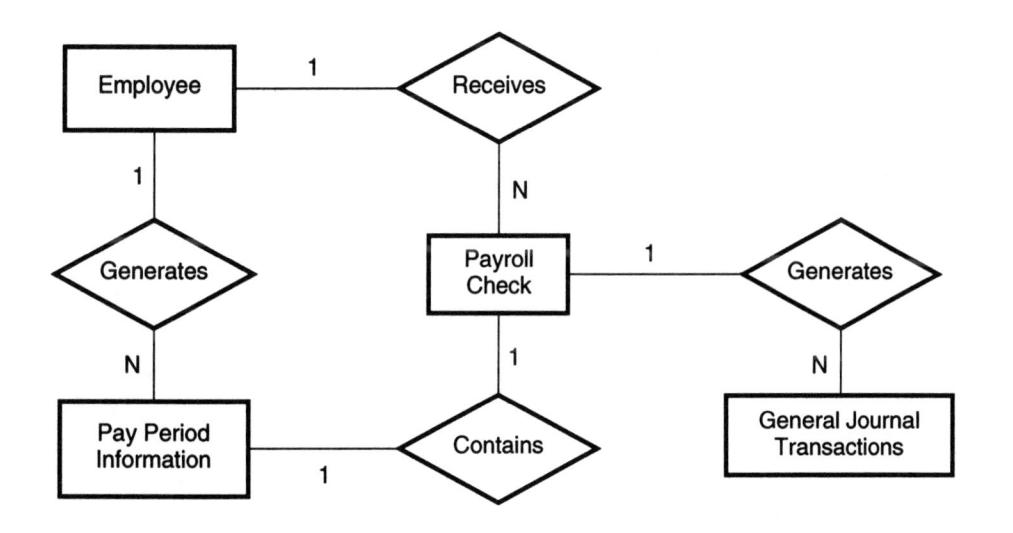

Figure 5-8
E-R Diagram for Payroll Related Functions

EXERCISES

1. Create unnormalized relations for the database in this case.
2. Normalize the relations to at least the third normal form.
3. Integrate this set of normalized relations with the set created of normalized relations from previous chapters. Re-normalize the integrated set of relations as required.
4. Create a data structure diagram for the database in this case following the format given in the textbook.

5. Using the volumes given in the case, calculate an estimate of the size of the database.
6. Draw logical access maps (LAMs) and database action diagrams (DADs) for each user view presented in the case.
7. Map the conceptual model of the database to the hierarchical, network, and relational logical models.
8. Write the SQL statements necessary to implement the database and the user views shown in the case.
9. Write the QBE statements necessary to implement the database and the user views shown in the case
10. Implement the database, add sample data, and produce user views shown in the case using an available SQL or QBE DBMS.
11. Create a data dictionary for the case.

PART II

Team Cases

CHAPTER 6 Celestial Customer Services
CHAPTER 7 Bedrock Builders, Inc.
CHAPTER 8 Eastrim County Supervisors

Part II contains three chapters, each presenting a unique and separate case. Each case discusses an organization that has a set of needs that ties into, but goes well beyond, the general accounting scenarios presented for Honest Computers Unlimited in Chapters 1 through 5.

Each of the three cases in Part II incorporates information elements for decision support. As a result, each case is based on fundamental transaction processing concepts. However, each case also includes requirements either for extracted information or for predictive information.

Celestial Customer Services is the subject organization of Chapter 6. Celestial was founded as a computer service bureau specializing in customer account billing services for a variety of clients. The company's computer system has been based on a file processing approach. In preparing to expand its services, the company has decided to convert its billing system to a database approach. The reader of this case might find it beneficial to review Chapters 1, 2, and 3, as they present similar concepts.

Celestial Customer Services is also planning to act on many customer requests to expand its services to include support for marketing activities. It is in that regard that the case expands to include features on which to build capabilities of a decision support system. The support of marketing activities, as requested by Celestial's clients, requires expanding the database to include information elements that allow for analysis of relationships among transaction, demographic, and opinion data and to make decisions that are of a predictive nature.

Bedrock Builders, Inc. is a residential construction firm that serves as a general home building contractor. It also subcontracts its framing crew to other general home construction companies. As the housing market slows down and the competition for construction loans gets tighter, Bedrock Builders needs to track its construction costs more accurately and to improve its processes for bidding on new construction projects. The details of that case are discussed in Chapter 7. A review of Chapters 1, 2, and 4 could prove beneficial to the reader of this case, as those chapters address similar concepts.

Bedrock Builders requires information to support decision making that differs from the needs discussed in other cases. Bedrock needs to examine what the impact of changes in price of labor and materials would be on the projected total cost of a construction project. The firm needs the capability to perform extensive "what if" analyses. The amount of additional data elements required to support that type of decision making is less than that needed by Celestial.

The County Supervisors of Eastrim County are elected by the voters of the county to manage activities of the county that are not specifically the domain of other elected officials. That includes overseeing the county's budget-related activities and administering Eastrim County's personnel policies. Chapter 8 deals with the computerized database requirements needed by the professional staff to carry out their duties for the County Supervisors. Chapters 1, 4, and 5 contain related information that might assist the reader of this case.

The decision support aspects of the Eastrim County case are quite different from those of the Celestial and Bedrock cases. The information elements required for the budget-related decisions are virtually the same set of elements as are required for the support of the transaction processing related to budget activities. In that sense, the decision support for the budget process is more similar to Bedrock than that of Celestial. However, in the support of personnel, related decisions, Eastrim County exhibits decision support needs that require qualitative text-based information in addition to the more quantitative data needed to support the other examples of decision making illustrated in these cases.

CHAPTER 6

Celestial Customer Services

INTRODUCTION

Nearly two decades ago, Billie Caplan founded Celestial Customer Services as a part-time, home-based business. In the beginning, she had three clients. Each was a small retail business that offered charge accounts to qualified customers. Each of her clients lacked the expertise to computerize their customer billing at the end of each month, so Billie provided that service for her clients.

Now, Celestial Customer Services has more than 200 clients for whom it performs services related to customer billing. Celestial's staff has grown to the equivalent of 24 full-time employees. Several employees are part-timers who each share one full-time position with one or two other workers.

Celestial's clientele represents several lines of business, including several retail companies and several wholesale firms. Celestial also has a few doctors' and dentists' practices as clients. More recent additions to the client list were five health/fitness clubs, two small independent business colleges, and seven utility companies. The latter category includes four privately owned landfill operations and was expected to grow rapidly due to much recent government regulation.

Each client provides copies of sales tickets, sales invoices or lists of sales, as well as payment receipts from which Celestial's data entry personnel input sales and receipts data. Typically, the source documents are delivered once a month, although some of the clients deliver their sales and receipts documents weekly. Celestial enters a client's sales and receipts data, updates the client's customer accounts, produces and mails statements of account to customers, and generates reports for the clients—all within three days of receiving the client's source documents.

Initially, each time Billie Caplan took on a new client in a new line of business, she paid an independent software company to write a new accounts receivable package. Now she realizes that she had paid them to "reinvent the wheel" several times with only minor variations being made each time. The cost of maintaining several similar software packages has gotten out of hand. She has wanted to correct that problem for several months but had not yet found an appropriate occasion to do so—that is, until now.

Recently, Billie has received inquiries from a few of her clients for Celestial to do more with the customer data. Each of the conversations revolved around the idea to use customer data in order to support the client's marketing efforts. Mostly, the clients wanted to conduct surveys of their customers' opinions with Celestial sending out the surveys, tabulating the data, and reporting the results.

Billie agreed to explore the idea and that Celestial would probably offer such marketing support services as long as it was profitable to do so. The cost of the services would be billed to Celestial's clients on the same time and charges basis as the billing services have been billed. That is, the client would pay a charge for data to be entered, for computer time and supplies used, and for spot-checking reports for accuracy.

Consultants advised Billie not to attempt to offer the new marketing support services unless the data was to be housed in a database. She saw this as the opportunity she had been waiting for to modernize and consolidate the several disjointed billing packages presently in place. She also realized that the conversion from a file processing approach would solve the software maintenance dilemma that Celestial has been facing.

Billie was also advised that Celestial Computer Services should continue to use a CPA firm for its own general ledger and payroll activities. She had no qualms with that notion as those were not her areas of expertise. She would continue to use Celestial's capabilities to bill its own clients at the end of each month for services rendered. The same billing software was used for that purpose as was used to process the data for Celestial's clients in the medical profession.

USER VIEWS: BILLING SERVICES

As previously indicated, the data for each type of client was processed using a different custom-written billing software package. Therefore, each line of business uses a different customer statement. So as to provide as little disruption as possible in the billing of its clients' customers, Celestial Customer Services will retain the formats for those customer statements.

Figures 6-1 through 6-6 show the six different statements that have been produced for the six lines of business which Celestial's clients represent. Figure 6-1 shows the statement for retail and wholesale companies. Figure 6-2 is the statement for medical practices. The customer statement sent to health and fitness clubs is illustrated by Figure 6-3. Both small private business schools use the statement contained in Figure 6-4. Gas, electric, and water utility companies use a statement as shown in Figure 6-5. Figure 6-6 presents the customer billing statement used by private landfill operators.

Billie Caplan wanted to standardize the user views that would be used as the data entry input screen for all of Celestial's clients. That is to say, she hopes to have one input screen to use to input all clients' sales user views and another for all clients' receipts data. That would make the data entry process more efficient,

Continued on page 47

WHOLESALE PLUMBING SUPPLY COMPANY
84 INDUSTRIAL PARK ROAD
WAGON MOUND, MONTANA 9999

STATEMENT OF CUSTOMER ACCOUNT

CUSTOMER NUMBER: 10111   STATEMENT DATE: June 30, 1994

CUSTOMER NAME: Carol's Custom Kitchens

BILLING ADDRESS: SHIPPING ADDRESS:
P.O. Box 3947   8147 Lookout Roa
Utah City, Utah 55555   Longgone, Utah 55556

DATE	REFERENCE	CHARGES	PAYMENTS	BALANCE
05/31/94	Beginning Balance			$1,230.00
06/04/94	Payment on Account		$ 230.00	1,000.00
06/12/94	Invoice #876543	$310.00		1,310.00
06/12/94	Invoice #87654	49.99		1,359.99
06/12/94	Payment on Account		1,059.99	300.00
06/30/94	Finance Charge	45.00		345.00

PLEASE PAY THE LAST AMOUNT IN THE BALANCE COLUMN WITHIN TEN DAYS

CURRENT	OVER 30 DAYS	OVER 60 DAYS	OVER 90 DAYS	OVER 120 DAYS
45.00	.00	.00	300.00	.00

Figure 6-1
User View 6-1: Customer statement for retail/wholesale companies.

STATEMENT OF ACCOUNT

FAMILY MEDICINE, P.C.
MEDICAL ARTS CENTER
SUITE 14
CHICAGO, IOWA 55515

JAYNE PLEASANT, M.D.
JAI SIRISAN, M.D.

RESPONSIBLE PARTY:

ACCOUNT NUMBER: 2345

Leonard Reynolds
84367 Fantasia Way
Apt. #43D
Chicago, Iowa 55515

STATEMENT DATE: 11/03/94

SERVICE DATE	DIAG. CODE	PATIENT NAME	SERVICE LOCATION	DESCRIPTION	CHARGE/ PATIENT	PAYMENT/ADJ. INSURANCE
10/01/94				BALANCE FORWARD:	$220.00	
10/05/94				payment		$120.00 CR
10/13/94	99201	Leo Jr.	Office	office visit	35.00	
10/13/94	87081	Leo Jr.	Office	strep screen	12.00	
10/13/94	86032	Leo Jr.	Office	antibody screen	5.00	
10/13/94	11523	Leo Jr.	Office	laceration	24.00	
10/13/94				payment		20.00 CR
10/21/94	73610	Leo Jr.	E.R.	ankle x ray	75.00	
10/21/94	99202	Leo Jr.	E.R.	exam	45.00	
10/21/94	85130	Leo Jr.	E.R.	cast	112.00	
10/25/94				payment		56.00 CR
10/27/94	99201	Alice	Office	office visit	35.00	
10/27/94	84703	Alice	Office	pregnancy test	12.00	
10/27/94				payment		5.00 CR
10/30/94				payment		232.00 CR
11/03/94		finance charge on balance over 30 days			14.00	

NEW BALANCE: $156.00

	TOTAL	PATIENT	INSURANCE
MONTH CHARGES	369.00	369.00	.00
MONTH PAYMENTS	433.00	25.00	408.00

BALANCE ANALYSIS

CURRENT	OVER 30 DAYS	OVER 60 DAYS	OVER 90 DAYS	OVER 120 DAYS
56.00	.00	100.00	.00	.00

Figure 6-2

User View 6-2: Customer statement for medical practices.

44 Part II Team Cases

```
FIRM BODIES FITNESS AND FUN CENTER
BROWSERS SHOPPING MALL
15TH AND STATE STREETS              "YOUR ONE STOP FITNESS SHOP"
VALLEY VIEW, CO  82999
1-555-FIRMBOD

                    STATEMENT OF MEMBER'S ACCOUNT
                           September 30, 1994

MEMBER:   Lanna Lumpe                ACCOUNT #  435
          1422 State Stree           PHONE NUMBERS:
          Apt. #4                    Home: (303) 555-1234
          Valley View, CO  82999     Work: (303) 555-6789
```

MEMBERSHIP INFORMATION   TYPE: Individual

INITIAL MEMBERSHIP FEE: $ 600.00   BEGINNING DATE: 9/30/93

FINANCED FOR: 24 months AT: 5%   TOTAL AMOUNT FINANCED: $ 660.00

RESULTING IN MONTHLY PAYMENTS OF: $ 27.50

DATE	DESCRIPTION	CHARGE	PAYMENT	BALANCE
09/01/94	Balance forward			$ 32.50
09/05/94	Guest visit - basic service	$10.00		
09/08/94	Payment on account		$32.50	
09/12/94	Guest visit - special service	20.00		
09/12/94	Vitamin and supplement package	35.00		
09/15/94	New member recruitment credit		50.00	
09/20/94	Massage and pedicure	25.00		
09/25/94	Strength consultation	12.00		
09/25/94	Credit for returned vitamins		15.00	
09/30/94	Monthly membership payment	27.50		
09/30/94	Monthly locker rental	5.00		

End of month balance $ 69.50

REMEMBER TO PAY YOUR ACCOUNT BALANCE BY THE TENTH OF NEXT
MONTH TO AVOID DISRUPTION OF YOUR MEMBERSHIP SERVICES

Figure 6-3
User View 6-3: Customer statement for health and fitness clubs.

MIDTOWN SCHOOL OF COMMERCE

"EXCELLENCE IN EDUCATION

FOR MORE THAN A QUARTER OF A CENTURY"

A. T. HELMS, SR., PRESIDENT   196 BELL CURVE
A. T. HELMS, JR., DEAN OF STUDENTS   WATERTOWN, CO 88888
A. T. HELMS III, REGISTRAR   718-555-6789

STATEMENT OF STUDENT ACCOUNT

STUDENT: Philip Gordon   STUDENT ID #: 555-66-7777

LOCAL ADDRESS: PERMANENT ADDRESS:
254 Student Residence Hall   33246 Long Street
Midtown School of Commerce   Apt. G42
Watertown, CO 88888   Raytown, NJ 01111

DATE	DESCRIPTION		CHARGE	CREDIT
01/05/94	Spring semester residence hall fee		$3,000.00	
01/05/94	Spring semester dining plan B		1,500.00	
01/15/94	Spring semester registration fee		50.00	
01/15/94	BUS201 Business Math	3 cr hrs	150.00	
01/15/94	ACC250 Intro to Accounting	3 cr hrs	150.00	
01/15/94	BUS271 Management Principles	3 cr hrs	150.00	
01/15/94	MIS181 Business Computers	4 cr hrs	200.00	
01/15/94	SEC105 Keyboarding	1 cr hrs	50.00	
01/15/94	Facilities fee	14 cr hrs	140.00	
01/15/94	Computer rental		200.00	
01/15/94	Student activities fee	14 cr hrs	280.00	
01/15/94	Parking fee		200.00	
01/18/94	Dean's List tuition remission			$ 150.00
01/18/94	Vocational Rehabilitation payment			2,000.00
01/18/94	Student employment credits			200.00
		TOTALS:	$6,070.00	$2,350.00

BALANCE DUE BY 01/31/94: $ 3720.00

OTHER STUDENT INFORMATION:
MATRICULATION DATE: 08/20/92   EXPECTED GRADUATION: 05/25/96
HOME HIGH SCHOOL: Raytown (NJ) HS   CLASS STATUS: sophomore
TOTAL HOURS EARNED: 50   GRADE POINT AVERAGE: 3.56
PROGRAM OF STUDY: Business Administration
ADMISSION CODES: 1: aa   2: nd   3: bb   4: ex

Figure 6-4

User View 6-4: Customer statement for private business schools.

Figure 6-5
User View 6-5: Customer statement for utilities.

```
                    SMALLTOWN, NEW MEXICO
                    DEPARTMENT OF UTILITIES
                          TOWN HALL
                    SMALLTOWN, NEW MEXICO, 99999
                          (505) 555-0000
```

STATEMENT DATE: 08/15/94

ACCOUNT NUMBER: MEN2345

Ray Mendoza
245 Third Street
Smalltown, NM 99999

(505) 555-2345

OLD METER READING	NEW METER READING	UNITS USED	RATE	DESCRIPTION	AMOUNT
				PREVIOUS BALANCE	$ 42.40
				PAYMENT (08/01/94)	42.40 CR
431600	432800	1200	.010	water service	12.00
				sewer service	10.00
				trash collection	15.00
				w/s/t tax	1.85
				W/S/T SUBTOTAL	38.85
38871	39558	687	.080	electric service	54.96
				electric surcharge	5.50
				electric tax	3.02
				ELECTRIC SUBTOTAL	63.48
				TOTAL CHARGES	102.33

PLEASE PAY BY THE FIRST OF THE MONTH TO AVOID A FINANCE CHARGE.

YOUR ELECTRIC USAGE THIS PERIOD WAS 687 KWH.
YOUR AVERAGE MONTHLY ELECTRIC USAGE THIS YEAR WAS 523 KWH.
CONTACT TOWN HALL IF YOU ARE INTERESTED IN BUDGET BILLING.

```
                    STATEMENT OF ACCOUNT

BIG SKY COUNTY LANDFILL SERVICE
RICHARD BIG SKY, PROPRIETOR
R.R. 2, P.O. BOX 8449
SOUPAW, SOUTH DAKOTA  87999
(605) 555-9999

CUSTOMER:                              ACCOUNT NUMBER:   12345

Annabelle's Cleaning Service           STATEMENT DATE:   05/03/94
ATTENTION: Annabelle Ringling
8425 Middleground Road
Soupaw, SD  87999
```

DATE	WEIGHT/ VOLUME		DESCRIPTION	RATE	CHARGE
04/03/94			BALANCE FORWARD		$ 287.00
04/07/94			payment on account		287.00 CR
04/10/94	82	cans	empty paint containers	.10	8.20
04/10/94	68	lbs	soiled varnish rags	.25	17.00
04/13/94	255	lbs	used wall board	.10	25.50
04/13/94	122	lbs	old fiber insulation	1.00	122.00
04/13/94	300	lbs	used pine lumber	.05	15.00
04/13/94	30	lbs	used nails	.10	3.00
04/23/94	30	gal	old formaldehyde	2.00	60.00
05/03/94			NEW BALANCE		$ 250.70

PAYMENT MUST BE RECEIVED BY THE FIFTEENTH OF THE MONTH
IN ORDER FOR SERVICE TO CONTINUE BEYOND THAT DATE.

Figure 6-6

User View 6-6: Customer statement for private landfill operators.

which translates to increased profits for Celestial Customer Services.

On initial examination, that might seem an unwise decision. However, one ought to remember that the data entry clerks at Celestial are merely entering data from customer-provided source documents for sales and receipts. At the time the data is entered, the sales and receipts transactions are already complete. Therefore, the system does not need to verify balances or prices for inventory items. Indeed, client inventory data are not present on Celestial's computer system. Similarly, the system does not need to validate customer data. In essence, the data entry clerk at Celestial is merely entering entire lines of sales and receipts data, including any mistakes made by the clients.

Despite Billie's hope that one user view can suffice for entering sales data for all clients and another for entering all receipts data, those user views have not yet been designed. When designed, they would be labeled as User View 6-7 and User View 6-8. She is willing to concede that her hopes might not be achievable. In that case, a separate user view might be required for sales data entry for each type of client. Likewise, a separate user view might be required for receipts data entry for each type of client. If so, those would be labeled User Views 6-7a through 6-7f and 6-8a through 6-8f, respectively.

Figure 6-7
User View 6-7 or User Views 6-7a through 6-7f. (The reader should use the area above to design this user view, as indicated in the narrative.)

Figure 6-8
User View 6-8 or User Views 6-8a through 6-8f. (The reader should use the area above to design this user view, as indicated in the narrative.)

Celestial prepares a set of reports for each client after the client's customer statements have been produced. Those reports include a mirror listing of all customer statements in formats similar to User Views 6-1 through 6-6. Other standard reports produced are User View 6-9, a customer account listing similar in format to that shown in Figure 6-9, and User View 6-10, an aged analysis report of overdue accounts similar to that shown in Figure 6-10.

WHOLESALE PLUMBING SUPPLY COMPANY
CUSTOMER ACCOUNT LISTING
MARCH 3, 1994

CUSTOMER NUMBER/NAME	MONTH SALES	YTD SALES	MONTH PAYMENT	YTD PAYMNT	BALANCE
124654 Johnstone Bathrooms	210.00	1800.00	210.00	1800.00	0.00
432873 Doug Stone Construction	149.00	399.00	250.00	250.00	149.00
1096546 Mavis' Interior Decor	500.00	2500.00	.00	1500.00	1000.00
114345 Speakeasy Homes	2850.00	2850.00	.00	.00	2850.00
1118345 Kristof Konstruction	825.50	1825.50	1825.50	1825.50	0.00
345632 Courtyard Kitchens	200.00	800.00	200.00	200.00	600.00
489484 Stone Yard Builders	852.99	852.99	852.99	852.99	0.00
1048348 More Than Mortar	.00	.00	85.00	85.00	765.00
398720 Custom Homes, Inc.	543.50	8123.87	543.50	8123.87	0.00

Figure 6-9
User View 6-9: Customer account listing.

WHOLESALE PLUMBING SUPPLY COMPANY
AGED ANALYSIS OF OVERDUE ACCOUNTS
MAY 3, 1994

CUSTOMER ACCT/PHONE #/NAME /CONTACT PERSON	ACCOUNT BALANCE	31-60 DAYS/ 61-90 DAYS/ 91-120 DAYS/ OVER 120 DAYS	LAST PAYMENT DATE/ AMOUNT
1096546		500.00	
303-555-9999		.00	
Mavis' Interior Decor		.00	04/01/94
Mavis McBee	500.00	.00	500.00
114345		2850.00	
303-555-1111		.00	
Speakeasy Homes		.00	00/00/00
Dawn Goner	2850.00	.00	.00
345632		.00	
505-555-2222		600.00	
Courtyard Kitchens		.00	02/10/94
Court Yard	600.00	.00	200.00
1048348		.00	
308-555-1234		.00	
More Than Mortar		765.00	02/05/94
Rock Mason	765.00	.00	85.00

Figure 6-10

User View 6-10: Aged analysis of overdue customer accounts.

GENERAL DESIGN AND USER VIEWS OF THE MARKETING SUPPORT SYSTEM

Several of Celestial Customer Services' clients had approached Billie Caplan recently with an idea for an expanded service. Billie had told them of the pending change from file processing to the database approach and the corresponding improvement in the services that Celestial provides. The clients all envisioned the opportunity to get more out of the customer database than just billing and related reporting.

The clients saw the changes at Celestial as a chance to improve their support of their marketing efforts. Specifically, the clients wanted to be able to gather data regarding customer demographics and opinions and to correlate that demographic and opinion data with information regarding customers' purchasing behaviors. In that manner, the clients could measure customer satisfaction, track the success of sales campaigns, and analyze the demographic profile of typical customers.

Most of the clients who had talked to Billie about adding the marketing support capability also commented on another idea. They recognized that the demographic and opinion data housed in the database could come from businesses and individuals other than customers. That would allow the clients to measure the traits and opinions of those who were not customers, perhaps learning how to improve their products and services to expand their customer bases.

The survey method was preferred by Celestial's clients for use in gathering opinion data. The system that Celestial was to design should have the flexibility to allow each client to conduct multiple surveys using multiple survey instruments. Each instrument could be completely unique, or a survey instrument might contain some of the same questions that had appeared on one or more previous instruments. Clients all agreed that, while open-ended questions could provide more insight, it would be more logical to restrict the questions to those with multiple-choice or quantifiable answers.

After several discussions with advisors who had expertise in market research and database design, Billie developed a basic idea as to how to begin to design this new marketing support data. She decided that the following entities should be reflected in the database: questionnaire, survey, question, answer, subject (or interviewee or respondent), and responses given by subjects.

After mulling over several scenarios, Billie decided that the relationships among the entities could be summarized in the following statements. Each survey will involve the use of only one questionnaire, but any given questionnaire can be used for multiple surveys. Each questionnaire can contain one or more questions, and each question can appear on one or more questionnaires. Each question can contain one or more answers, and each answer can be used for one or more questions. The answers for any particular question can vary from one questionnaire to the next. A survey questionnaire can be administered to one or more subjects and any one subject can respond to one or more survey questionnaires. A subject can also respond to the same questionnaire on multiple occasions to allow for collection of data to reflect a longitudinal study. Therefore, dating the surveys and subjects' answers is very important.

As she thought more deeply about the nature of the subjects to whom the questionnaires would be administered, Billie arrived at the following notion. As stated previously, some of Celestial's clients wanted to gather data from subjects other than their customers. Therefore, it did not sound wise to include the survey data in the customer portion of the database. She decided that the better approach would be to use the principle of inheritance in an object-oriented sense. The ideal design would be to create or recognize an entity called "person," which would house the attributes related to all persons. Then the customer entity and the subject entity could each inherit the attributes from the person entity as appropriate.

That scheme would also allow Billie to pursue another idea at a future time. She realized that the collective size of all the clients' databases could grow rapidly as they begin to conduct surveys among the general public. Of course, the clients pay Celestial to maintain their data, so the cost factor associated with the purchase of sufficient disk capacity is covered. However, the cost associated with processing those huge databases might become counterproductive, especially as the system accesses multiple relations to link inherited data.

Billie seldom had difficulty persuading Celestial's clients to take advantage of cost-saving measures, especially when some of the savings was passed along to the clients. So, Billie figured that at a future time she could convince many of the clients to combine their person data, which most likely would have evolved to be greatly overlapping sets. That would allow any duplicate persons to be purged and would facilitate inheritance. It would also provide each client a larger pool of persons to tap when conducting a new survey. For those reasons, creating a person entity seemed to be the best approach.

Billie decided that the following user views would be required for the marketing support database. User View 6-11 would be a list of all general information associated with each survey. User View 6-12 would be a display of the questions and answers for a particular questionnaire. User View 6-13 would list all summary data for the questions used in a particular survey questionnaire. User View 6-14 would show the responses given by the subjects. User View 6-15 would show the information for occurrences of the person entity. Those user views are illustrated by Figures 6-11 through 6-15.

Billie also recognized that there would be appropriate user views for data entry to input new questions and answers and to record the responses of subjects. Those are not illustrated herein as they are quite simple and do not add any data elements that do not appear in other user views. The reader is encouraged to consider such user views.

Another set of views are not shown herein. Consultants predict that, after clients have mastered usage of User Views 6-11 through 6-15, they will begin to request many other views to allow them to examine the relationships among sales patterns and opinion/demographic data. A very large percentage of those views can be created using the query language of the chosen database management software package.

```
              FIRM BODIES FITNESS AND FUN CENTER
                    INFORMATION ABOUT SURVEYS
```

SURVEY NUMBER	BEGIN DATE /END DATE	INTERVIEWER	PURPOSE/ LOCATION	METHOD	QUESTION- NAIRE #
1	08/16/94 08/20/94	Fred Drews	measure success of new TV ad campaign mall	random stops	1
2	09/16/94 09/25/94	Fred Drews	measure success of new radio ads mall	random stops	2
3	11/16/94 11/20/94	Fred Drews	measure success of new TV ad campaign mall	random stops	1
4	12/15/94 12/23/94	several	promote Christmas specials office	random phone calls	3
5	02/16/95 02/20/95	Sally Smith	measure success of new radio ads mall	random stops	2
6	05/25/95 06/25/95	staff	gather opinions on customer service mailing	all customers	4
7	08/16/95 08/20/95	Sally Smith	measure success of new TV ad campaign mall	random stops	1
8	10/05/95	staff	preference data on competitive products mailing	random from phone book	5

et cetera

Figure 6-11

User View 6-11: Listing of data about surveys.

FIRM BODIES FITNESS AND FUN CENTER
QUESTIONNAIRE Q & A LIST
Questionnaire # 2

NAME:
ADDRESS:
CITY:
STATE:
COUNTRY:
ZIP OR POSTAL CODE:
PHONE #:

SEQUENCE NUMBER	QUESTION NUMBER	ANSWER NUMBER	QUESTIONS / ANSWERS
1	1		What kind of shape are you in?
		1	Very good
		2	Above average
		3	Average
		4	Not too good
		5	Pretty bad
2	2		What shape would you like to be in?
		1	Very good
		2	Above average
		3	Average
3	5		How frequently do you visit a health or fitness club?
		8	Daily
		9	Weekly
		10	Monthly
		11	Less frequently
		12	Never
4	7		Do you think you exercise or work out more frequently or less frequently than the average person?
		6	More frequently
		11	Less frequently

et cetera

User View 6-12
Display of questionnaire questions and answers.

```
┌─────────────────────────────────────────────────────────────────┐
│              FIRM BODIES FITNESS AND FUN CENTER                 │
│              SUBJECTS' RESPONSES TO QUESTIONNAIRE               │
│                                                                 │
│         SURVEY NUMBER:         2                                │
│                                                                 │
│   QUESTIONNAIRE NUMBER:        2                                │
│                                                                 │
│       DATE ADMINISTERED:    09/16/94 - 09/25/94                 │
│                                                                 │
│      NUMBER OF SUBJECTS:       50                               │
└─────────────────────────────────────────────────────────────────┘
```

	QUESTIONS/ANSWERS	N	WGHT	WGHT AVG	STD. DEV.
1	What kind of shape are you in?	49		2.94	.83
	Very good	5	1		
	Above average	5	2		
	Average	29	3		
	Not too good	8	4		
	Pretty bad	2	5		
2	What shape would you like to be in?	50		2.00	.40
	Very good	10	1		
	Above average	30	2		
	Average	10	3		
3	How frequently do you visit a health or fitness club?	50		4.06	1.22
	Daily	1	1		
	Weekly	5	2		
	Monthly	8	3		
	Less frequently	12	4		
	Never	24	5		
4	Do you think you exercise or work out more frequently or less frequently than the average person?	50		1.50	.25
	More frequently	25	1		
	Less frequently	25	2		

et cetera

Figure 6-13

User View 6-13: Summary of responses to questions.

FIRM BODIES FITNESS AND FUN CENTER
SUBJECTS' RESPONSES TO QUESTIONNAIRE

SURVEY NUMBER: 2

QUESTIONNAIRE NUMBER: 2

DATE ADMINISTERED: 09/20/94

SUBJECT (RESPONDENT): Bud Meister

1. What kind of shape are you in?

   Not too good

2. What shape would you like to be in?

   Above average

3. How frequently do you visit a health or fitness club?

   Never

4. Do you think you exercise or work out more frequently or less frequently than the average person?

   Less frequently

5. If cost was not an issue, how frequently would you attend a health or fitness club?

   Weekly

6. What have you heard about Firm Bodies Fitness and Fun Center?

   Very favorable comments

et cetera

Figure 6-14

User View 6-14: Subjects' responses to questionnaire.

FIRM BODIES FITNESS AND FUN CENTER

PERSON ENTITY LISTING

March 31, 1995

NAME/ NUMBER	STREET ADDRESS/ CITY/STATE/ZIP	HOME PHONE WORK PHONE
Bud Meister 12	123 Main Street Buffalo, WY 99991	307-555-1234 307-555-1235
Sally Doe 14	8312 Cravass Way Bison, WY 99991	307-555-9877 307-555-9878
Freeda Drews 15	47 Canterberry Road Bull, CO 89999	303-555-1234 719-555-1234
Fritz Katt 22	P.O. Box 76a Elk, UT 99990	801-555-1111 801-555-1112
Ian Jones 25	723 Central Avenue Huckey, CO 80999	303-555-1122 303-555-2211
Courtney Jones 30	1 Regency Court Road's End, CO 81999	719-555-6666 719-555-5555
Tyler Jones 32	43 Lower Street Downtown, IL 39999	312-555-7897 312-555-7987
Drew Tu 40	11234 Forever Road Anytown, WY 99999	307-555-9876 307-555-9867

et cetera

Figure 6-15

User View 6-15: Listing of data for the person entity.

STORAGE REQUIREMENTS

In her feasibility study on converting from the file processing approach to the database approach, Billie Caplan performed an analysis of the volumes of data that are managed by the old system and the volumes of data that would be managed by the new system. She calculated that Celestial's more than 200 clients have a cumulative total of approximately 10,000 customers. Each of the customers generates two sales transactions per month and each one generates one sales receipt per month on the average.

When the marketing support portion of the database is implemented, additional storage space will be required. As with any new application, this one is destined to begin slowly and then build. However, this particular application is being requested by the clients. Therefore, it will probably have a faster start than most new applications.

Eventually, there will be an estimated 1,000 questionnaires with an average of 20 questions each. Surveys will be administered at the rate of about 30 per month, and the person database should grow to nearly 20,000 entries who will have participated in the first three years of the new marketing support system. Each of those will have participated in approximately 10 surveys each.

If and when the clients are persuaded to combine the person portions of their databases, there will be some initial reduction in storage requirements. Billie estimates that 2-3,000 duplicate names will be deleted. However, she also estimates that reduction will be offset by growth within a few months.

The field sizes or attribute widths allocated on the user views contained in Figures 6-1 through 6-15 are a fairly good representation of the storage needs that should be allocated for the database.

EXERCISES

1. Draw a data flow diagram for the customer billing part of this case.
2. Draw a data flow diagram for the marketing support part of this case.
3. Draw an entity-relationship diagram for the customer billing portion of this case.
4. Draw an entity-relationship diagram for the marketing support portion of the case.
5. What are the advantages and disadvantages of having User Views 6-7 and 6-8 versus having User Views 6-7a through 6-7f and 6-8a through 6-8f, as explained in the case narrative?
6. Choose one of the options given in #5 and design the appropriate user views.
7. Create a set of unnormalized relations for the customer billing part of the database in this case.
8. Create a set of unnormalized relations for the marketing support part of the database in this case.
9. Normalize the marketing support relations to at least the third normal form.
10. Normalize the customer billing relations to at least the third normal form.
11. Integrate the customer billing set of normalized relations with the marketing support set of normalized relations. Re-normalize the integrated set of relations as required.
12. Create a data structure diagram for the database in this case following the format given in the textbook.
13. Using the volumes given in the case, calculate an estimate of the size of the database.
14. Draw logical access maps (LAMs) and database action diagrams (DADs) for each user view presented above.
15. Map the conceptual model of the database in this case to the IMS or other similar hierarchical model.
16. Map the conceptual model of the database in this case to the CODASYL network model.
17. Map the conceptual model of the database in this case to the relational model.
18. Write the SQL statements necessary to implement the database and the user views shown in this case.
19. Write the QBE statements necessary to implement the database and the user views shown in the case
20. Implement the database, add sample data, and produce user views shown in the case using an available SQL or QBE DBMS.
21. Create a data dictionary for the case.
22. Assume that Celestial wants to enhance its marketing support system by adding the capability to track sales prospects and the activities related to them. How would you accomplish this? What additional user views would be needed? Design those user views and draw unnormalized relations from them. Then normalize them to at least the third normal form. Integrate the relations with the other relations, data flow diagrams, entity–relationship diagrams, SQL or QBE implementation, and data dictionary.

CHAPTER 7

Bedrock Builders, Inc.

INTRODUCTION

Bedrock Builders, Inc. has earned a reputation for building quality homes for buyers in the middle-income range. Among other home builders, the firm is well known for completing projects on schedule and for staying within estimated construction costs. Both of those distinctions are quite gratifying to Bedrock Builders' president, Thor Bodily.

The reputation for quality is one that Bodily helped create. When he started as an apprentice carpenter during high school, the master carpenters under whom he worked insisted on paying proper attention to detail. They lived that philosophy and took great pride in being known as the best carpenters in the vicinity. That pride was infectious. Bodily caught it and, throughout his career, mentored young workers to help instill both attention to detail and the resulting pride.

Bodily's ability to motivate new employees is what caught Sam Bedrock's attention. As a fellow worker, he gained a respect for Bodily's talents. When Bedrock formed his own company, the first employee he hired was Bodily. He built his new company around those talents. It was chiefly due to Bodily's efforts that Bedrock Builders earned the reputation for quality.

Sam Bedrock's contribution to the new company was equally important. As a shrewd manager, he greatly refined his talent of closely estimating construction costs. That enabled him to be the lowest bidder on many profitable construction projects. Equally important was his ability to manage projects so they were completed on time and within the estimated costs. That part of the company's reputation was directly attributable to Sam Bedrock.

Both Bedrock and Bodily were amply rewarded for the critical roles they played in the success of Bedrock Builders. Bedrock paid himself well enough to retire rather early in life. Bodily was also well paid and was given a great deal of authority in the company. When Bedrock retired, he promoted Bodily to the position of president of the company. Sam Bedrock's other interests kept him occupied and away from the construction firm most of the time. He trusted Thor Bodily to run the company autonomously.

Thor Bodily's tenure as president started very well indeed. He was able to expand on his extraordinary ability to motivate construction workers. The company realized immediate productivity gains in the office staff and in the marketing associates.

Unfortunately, there was a hitch. Bodily soon learned that he did not have the same unique business sense that Bedrock possessed. He was not able to estimate costs so closely as to win important bids and still stay within cost and time estimates with the same precision as his predecessor. Obviously, he knew enough about construction to build a good bid. However, he lacked an ability to consistently — and seemingly effortlessly — generate great bids like Bedrock.

Thor Bodily seized the first available opportunity to quiz Sam Bedrock on his ability in regard to generating bids. Bedrock gave credit to his phenomenal talent to anticipate even the slightest changes in the cost of materials and labor. He pointed out that in the course of the three to five months that it takes to construct a medium-sized residence, dozens of changes in costs can and do occur. On a large project — say, the framing work on several homes in a new subdivision — changes can literally number in the hundreds. Many of the changes are slight, but the cumulative impact of all changes can consume a very large percentage of the planned profit for the project.

Sam Bedrock had many other interests and investments besides the construction company. He was an avid reader of financial news stories. He had many contacts in several different industries who shared information with him. As a direct result, Bedrock was able to foresee and plan for many of the small changes in costs that caught other home builders by surprise. Bodily began to realize what Sam had meant when he used to claim that all of his outside interests and investments contributed to make Bedrock Builders, Inc. a better company.

Bodily also realized that, if the company was to continue to deserve its reputation for superb job estimating, he would need to spend much more time keeping track of outside factors that influence the construction business. In order to make time for that critical success factor as well as to continue to spend the needed time to serve as the motivational leader, certain changes had to take place.

Specifically, Thor Bodily realized he needed help with the paperwork associated with the bid process. He required the ability to quickly — and often at the last minute — make small cost changes to a bid. The process was an ideal computer application.

He sought advice from local computer dealers, who envisioned Bedrock Builders' needs as a typical spreadsheet application. The sales representatives from several of those companies praised the "what if" capability of spreadsheet software. They touted that capability as the perfect solution to the problem at hand.

On the other hand, one computer salesperson whom Bodily consulted argued persuasively that Bedrock's was really a database application. The same ability for sensitivity analysis could be achieved through the use of database software. Plus, the database approach could provide benefits that would be difficult to garner with spreadsheet software. (The sales rep stated that she had seen the light in a multi-user oriented database class she had taken in college.)

The key to the benefits that use of a database could provide was that the data for job bidding purposes could be tied relatively easily to the activities involved with tracking costs on existing jobs. Database software could also be used to extract reports in a wide variety of formats, a more difficult task to accomplish using spreadsheet software.

After verifying the saleswoman's claims with a few database experts, Bodily decided on the database approach to solve the problem at Bedrock Builders, Inc. He decided that the job cost tracking processes would be the first to be computerized. As soon as the computerization of that application was completed, the company would undertake the computerization of the job bidding processes. The rationale for that order is that the job bidding application needs to use historical information generated from the job tracking system.

If all goes well, Bodily plans to consider computerizing other applications, such as inventory control, sales and accounts receivable, accounts payable and check writing, payroll, and general ledger, at a later date. Until then, Bedrock Builders, Inc. would continue to use the services of a CPA firm for the payroll and general ledger applications. Sales and accounts receivable, at present, are quite simple as the market and Bedrock's reputation are such that most of their houses are presold through real estate companies that interface with the customers and handle all the details of each sale. Likewise, accounts payable and check writing are not a big chore, as Bedrock obtains a construction loan for each project and the conditions of the loan specify that the lender — usually a savings and loan company — will directly pay suppliers as expenses accrue. The need for a computerized inventory control system is limited, at present, due to the direct shipment of materials to job sites, as explained in the next section.

USER VIEWS: JOB COST TRACKING

Purchases from vendors are the source of transactions that feed the job cost tracking system. When Bedrock Builders purchases goods from a wholesaler, the wholesaler — such as a lumberyard or an electrical supply house — ships ordered materials to a specified address for a particular home construction project. Only the items shipped to that address for that project are contained on the accompanying invoice from the wholesale firm. That makes it easier for Bedrock to track costs separately by project. Suppliers provide that service only if Bedrock Builders segregates its materials orders by job.

One concern that arises is whether this approach would require Bedrock to forfeit any discounts that are based on quantity of materials purchased. In recognition of this concern and in order to stimulate repeat business, many of the suppliers offer progressive discounts based on the total purchases from a customer in a given time period. Consequently, the more business a contractor does with a supplier in a month, quarter, or year, the greater the discount rate on the next purchase.

There are six user views that comprise the job cost tracking system. User view 7-1 is a list of materials that Bedrock Builders gives to the wholesale company. Typically, that view is a handwritten shopping list with the items required and a quantity for each. For example, one list might indicate "346 - 8 ft pine studs, 10 lb of 3" nails, and 12 - 16 ft pine 2x4s." The lists are prepared by job supervisors or by whoever in the office answers phone calls from job supervisors. Bodily checks each list for reasonableness before it goes to the vendor. Most suppliers will take orders over the phone although some require a personal visit. As indicated by Figure 7-1, that user view is left to the reader to devise.

Figure 7-1
User View 7-1: Shopping List of Needed Materials. (The reader should use the area above to design this user view, as indicated in the narrative.)

The second user view is the invoice supplied by the wholesale company. Each supplier can have a uniquely formatted invoice. A typical vendor invoice is shown in Figure 7-2.

The third user view is a computer display used to input data for the job tracking system. This user view is shown in Figure 7-3. One vendor invoice at a time is entered using the entry display. The computer opera-

---

BOB'S BUILDER SUPPLY COMPANY

5692 East North Access Road

Waterville, Illinois 60606

CUSTOMER INVOICE

INVOICE NUMBER: 3896756
CUSTOMER NUMBER: 1624
ORDER DATE: 07/18/96
SHIPMENT DATE: 07/20/96

CUSTOMER: Bedrock Builders, Inc.
Attention: Thor Bodily
P.O. Box 4448
Waterville, Illinois 60606
(999) 555-9999

SHIP TO: 1776 Patriot Way
ORDER TAKEN FROM: Thor Bodily   VIA: phone
CURRENT BALANCE: $ .00   PURCHASES YTD: $ 285,125.94

QUANTITY	UNITS	ITEM NUMBER	ITEM DESCRIPTION	PRICE	UNIT EXTENSION
346	ln ft	12544	8 ft pine studs	.10	$ 276.80
10	lb	34563	3" nails	1.69	16.90
12	ln ft	167845	16 ft pine 2x4s	.24	46.08

SUBTOTAL: $ 339.78
5% SALES TAX: 16.99
DELIVERY CHARGE: 20.00
GROSS AMOUNT: $ 376.77
DISCOUNT @ EARNED RATE OF 9 %: 33.91
NET AMOUNT: $ 342.86

ALL INVOICES ARE PAYABLE WITHIN 30 DAYS OF DELIVERY DATE
PLEASE PAY ON TIME TO CONTINUE TO RECEIVE YOUR EARNED DISCOUNT

THANK YOU FOR YOUR BUSINESS!

Figure 7-2
User View 7-2: Sample Invoice from Supplier

tor types in a job number that has been handwritten on the vendor invoice after it was received in the Bedrock Builders' office. The job number tells the system to call up and display the corresponding job address so the operator can verify that the invoice should be attributed to that job. If any of that data is incorrect, the system allows the operator to type the correct data. Then the operator types in a delivery date, and the system moves to the body of the input form. In the body, the operator types in the quantity, description, and cost of the material being purchased and a number to indicate the job category to which the cost should be charged. The name of that cost category is displayed by the system to allow the operator to verify that the proper cost category number was entered. After the last line, the system calculates an invoice total to allow the vendor to verify that the data has been entered properly. If not, the system allows the operator to correct the data before proceeding to the next invoice.

User view 7-4 is a printed or displayed summary listing for each active construction job, as illustrated by Figure 7-4. It shows static information for each job, i.e., job name and number, as well as job inception and estimated completion dates. For each category of each job, it also shows the purchase activity for the period, the total for the period, the total since the inception of the job, and the budgeted amount for the category. A printed copy of this user view is given to the lender as a "draw report" along with the stack of invoices for the lender to pay.

The fifth user view is also a report that can be either printed or displayed. The format of user view 7-5 is similar to that of user view 7-4. The differences between the two user views lie in the detail data that the views contain. Whereas user view 7-4 shows the detail for a particular period for a particular job, user view 7-5 shows the detail for a particular period for all jobs. The reader should be able to design user view 7-5, as indicated by Figure 7-5.

User view 7-6 is also a summary report that can be printed or displayed. It is a listing of all jobs, showing the total expenditures, budgets, and amounts remaining to be spent as well as the percentage remaining. It is shown in Figure 7-6.

VENDOR INVOICE/JOB DATA ENTRY DISPLAY

JOB NUMBER: 4356
JOB ADDRESS: 1776 Patriot Way
DELIVERY DATE: 07/20/96

QUANTITY	ITEM DESCRIPTION	COST	JOB CATEGORY	CATEGORY NAME
346	8 ft pine studs	276.80	10	framing - wood
10	3" nails	16.90	12	framing - other
12	16 ft pine 2x4s	46.08	10	framing - wood
1	sales tax	16.99	96	taxes
1	delivery charge	20.00	97	delivery
1	purchase discount	-33.91	99	discounts
		342.86		

Figure 7-3
User View 7-3: Vendor Invoice/Job Data Entry Display

```
                    JOB DETAIL LISTING/DRAW REPORT
                          07/15/96 - 07/30/96

           JOB NUMBER:        4356
           JOB ADDRESS:       1776 Patriot Way
        INCEPTION DATE:       07/05/96
ESTIMATED COMPLETION DATE:    09/01/96
```

JOB CATEGORY	CATEGORY NAME	DATE	AMOUNTS	PERIOD TOTAL	JOB TOTAL	JOB BUDGET
01	land				13,500.00	13,500.00
03	excavating				1300.00	1300.00
05	foundation - labor				285.00	300.00
06	foundation - material				1250.00	1500.00
10	framing - wood	07/15	285.00			
		07/20	276.80			
		07/20	46.08	607.88	607.88	600.00
11	framing - trusses	07/25	2386.00	2386.00	2386.00	2400.00
12	framing - other	07/20	16.90	16.90	16.90	30.00
etc.						
			TOTALS:	33,085.91	33,085.91	78,000.00

Figure 7-4

User View 7-4: Job Detail Listing/Draw Report

Figure 7-5

User View 7-5: Cost Category Detail for All Jobs. (The reader should use the area above to design this user view, as indicated in the narrative.)

SUMMARY INFORMATION FOR ALL JOBS
as of 07/30/96

Status	JOB #	JOB ADDRESS	TOTAL SPENT	%	BUDGET	AMOUNT REMAINING
c	2335	120 Regency Loop	70,021.00	100.00	70,000.00	21.00-
c	2876	123 Main Street	68,000.95	104.62	65,000.00	3,000.95-
c	3572	8594 Know Way	72,185.00	96.25	75,000.00	2,815.00
a	4356	1776 Patriot Way	33,085.91	42.42	78,000.00	44,914.09
i	4358	1778 Patriot Way	14,800.00	18.97	78,000.00	63,200.00
i	4359	1780 Patriot Way	13,300.00	17.05	78,000.00	64,700.00
a	4700	no address yet	15,000.00	20.00	75,000.00	60,000.00
etc.						

Status: c = complete, a = active, i = inactive

Figure 7-6
User View 7-6: Summary Information for All Jobs

GENERAL DESIGN AND USER VIEWS OF THE JOB BIDDING SYSTEM

After the job cost tracking system has been successfully implemented and executed for a few accounting cycles, Thor Bodily will initiate the implementation of the job estimating subsystem. The latter system will use data from the former system. Hence, it is logical to defer installation of the job estimation system.

The motivation to implement a job estimating system is to assist Bodily as he attempts to continue Bedrock's tradition of generating precise and profitable job estimates. There are two major aspects involved in that mission. One is to closely follow events that could in any way affect prices of materials that comprise a bid for a residential construction project. Bodily figures that will consume a very large proportion of his time. The other aspect is the ability to quickly recalculate job estimates based on those actual and anticipated changes. It is in the latter respect that "what-if" capabilities of a computerized job estimating system will be a great benefit.

The job estimating system will utilize the concept of "standard jobs." There are a few basic floor plans or sets of blueprints from which Bedrock Builders typically builds. Most of the residential structures that Bedrock constructs stem from one of those few basic starting points. Bedrock's basic floor plans are relatively easy to modify. Therefore, variations from the basic jobs can usually be incorporated with minimal effort.

Each of the basic floor plans will be set up as a standard job. Associated with each of the standard jobs will be the list of items — known as a bill of materials — required to construct that residence. The bill of materials will include the quantities and descriptions of each of the job categories that comprise a finished house.

In order to make the system work properly, there must be a standard cost associated with each job category. That is to say, there will be a standard cost entered for framing lumber, copper pipe, electrical wiring, and all other job categories that Bedrock uses to build houses. Also associated with each job category will be a multiplier, which is a factor used to record any real or projected temporary change in the cost of the category. The multiplier will facilitate the what-if analysis. Permanent changes in costs will be reflected by changing the job category's cost rather than the multiplier.

There also needs to be a multiplier associated with groups or classes of job categories. That will allow what-if analysis to be performed at a level higher than that of individual job category. Thus, as Bodily prepares a bid on a particular construction project, he can perform his analysis of costs by changing the price for any given job category, by changing the multiplier for any given job category, by changing the multiplier for classes or groups of items, or by changing a multiplier associated with the overall standard job.

His analysis might also necessitate changing the job categories that comprise the standard job or the units of one or more of the job categories. The system will also allow Bodily to save any of the changes he makes by creating a variation of the standard job. Any such saved variation can then be recalled and manipulated separately from the standard job that was its source.

There are six user views required to implement the job estimating system. The first of those, user view 7-7, is the computer display that allows data to be input regarding individual job category. That data includes the number and name of the category as well as the standard cost and multiplier. That user view is shown in Figure 7-7.

User views 7-8 and 7-9 are similar to each other, as indicated by Figures 7-8 and 7-9. The former allows for a computer operator to specify data about a standard job, including which job categories comprise the standard job and the multiplier for the job. The latter allows for the same specifications to be stated for a grouping or class of job categories.

User view 7-10 (see Figure 7-10) is the view Bodily will use to perform his what-if analysis. He will be able to change any of the permanent job category units and costs and any of the multipliers. He will be able to immediately see the impact on any job category for any standard job. He will also be able to see immediately the impact on the total projected cost for a specified job.

Figure 7-11 illustrates user view 7-11, which is the computer display that Bodily will use to create a new job as a variation on any old job. He will probably learn to use this view to create a new job and then perform what-if analysis on the newly created job rather than on the standard job itself. That would create less risk of inadvertently corrupting a standard job.

The last user view, 7-12, is a report that can be either displayed or printed. It is shown in Figure 7-12. The report lists the estimated costs for all job categories for any particular job. This is the report that is printed and submitted as a job bid sheet after all the costs have been updated and all the what-if analysis has been completed.

JOB CATEGORY

DATA INPUT SCREEN

[If job category number already exists, the system will display data for that number and allow operator to change it.]

CATEGORY NUMBER: 10

CATEGORY NAME: framing - wood

STANDARD COST: $ 0.10

MULTIPLIER: 1.000

Figure 7-7

User View 7-7: Job Category Data Input Screen

Figure 7-8

User View 7-8: Standard Job Data Input Screen

```
                    STANDARD JOB
                  DATA INPUT SCREEN

STANDARD JOB NUMBER:   101

  STANDARD JOB NAME:   La Vista ranch w/basement

      JOB MULTIPLIER:  1.000


JOB CATEGORY # 1:    10      NAME:  framing - wood         QUANTITY:  464

JOB CATEGORY # 2:    03      NAME:  excavating             QUANTITY:    1

JOB CATEGORY # 3:    11      NAME:  framing - trusse       QUANTITY:   36

JOB CATEGORY # 4:    01      NAME:  land                   QUANTITY:    1

                    etc.

JOB CATEGORY # n:    06      NAME:  foundation - material  QUANTITY:  108
```

Figure 7-9

User View 7-9: Job Category Class Data Input Screen

```
                   JOB CATEGORY CLASS
                   DATA INPUT SCREEN

     JOB CATEGORY CLASS:   2000

     JOB CATEGORY NAME:    lumber

JOB CATEGORY MULTIPLIER:   1.200


    JOB CATEGORY # 1:    10    NAME:  framing - wood

    JOB CATEGORY # 2:    11    NAME:  framing - trusses

    JOB CATEGORY # 3:    31    NAME:  flooring - wood

    JOB CATEGORY # 4:    43    NAME:  interior woodwork


                    etc.


    JOB CATEGORY # n:    66    NAME:  exterior facet
```

```
                    WHAT-IF ANALYSIS SCREEN


    JOB NUMBER:    2368

      JOB NAME:    La Vista ranch w/basement

  JOB MULTIPLIER: 1.000


  CATEGORY                      QUANTITY        COST         MULTIPLIER
  # 1:    10    framing - wood      464         371.20          1.000

  # 2:    03    excavating           1        1,950.00          1.500

  # 3:    11    framing - trusses   36          900.00          1.000

  # 4:    0     land                 1       13,500.00          1.350


                       etc.


  # n:    06    foundation - material  108    1,080.00          1.000
                                              ─────────
                        TOTAL COST:           78,885.65
                                              ═════════
```

Figure 7-10
User View 7-10: What-If Analysis Screen

```
              JOB REPLICATION SCREEN


              JOB TO BE REPLICATED:

  JOB NUMBER:  2368

    JOB NAME:  La Vista ranch w/basement



                RESULTING JOB:

  JOB NUMBER:  8546

    JOB NAME:  847 Northface Blvd.
```

Figure 7-11
User View 7-11: Job Replication Screen

JOB BID SHEET

JOB NUMBER: 8546

BASIC DESIGN: La Vista ranch w/basement

JOB LOCATION: 847 Northface Blvd.

CATEGORY	QUANTITY	COST
framing - wood	464	371.20
excavating	1	1,950.00
framing - trusses	36	900.00
land	1	13,500.00
etc.		
foundation - material	108	1,080.00
TOTAL BID:		$ 78,885.65

Figure 7-12
User View 7-12: Job Bid Sheet

STORAGE REQUIREMENTS

In his feasibility study on implementing the job cost tracking system, Thor Bodily performed an analysis of the volumes of data that will be included in the new systems. He calculated that there are normally about 100 open jobs against which costs could be charged. Each job has an average of 50 cost categories. There are approximately 500 invoices from suppliers each month with an average of seven lines per invoice.

When the job estimating portion of the database is implemented, additional storage space will be required. As with any new application, this one is destined to begin slowly and then build. However, Bodily is anxious for this application to be implemented. Therefore, it will probably have a faster start than most new applications.

In the beginning, there will be 30 standard jobs with an average of 50 job categories per job. Eventually there will be an estimated 1000 job estimates or modifications of the standard jobs on file.

The field sizes or attribute widths allocated on the user views contained in Figures 7-1 through 7-12 are a fairly good representation of the storage needs that should be allocated for the database.

EXERCISES

1. Draw a data flow diagram for the job cost tracking part of this case.
2. Draw a data flow diagram for the job estimating part of this case.
3. Draw an entity-relationship diagram for the job cost tracking part of the case.
4. Draw an entity-relationship diagram for the job estimating part of the case.
5. Design appropriate user views for views 7-1 and 7-5.
6. Create a set of unnormalized relations for the job cost tracking part of the database in this case.
7. Create a set of unnormalized relations for the job estimating part of the database in this case.
8. Normalize the job cost tracking relations to at least the third normal form.
9. Normalize the job estimating relations to at least the third normal form.
10. Integrate the job cost tracking set of normalized relations with the job estimating set of normalized relations. Re-normalize the integrated relations as required.
11. Create a data structure diagram for the database in this case following the format given in the text.
12. Using the volumes given in the case, calculate the size of the database.
13. Draw logical access maps (LAMs) and database action diagrams (DADs) for each user view presented above.
14. Map the conceptual model of the database in this case to the IMS or other similar hierarchical model.
15. Map the conceptual model of the database in this case to the CODASYL network model.
16. Map the conceptual model of the database in this case to the relational model.
17. Write the SQL statements necessary to implement the database and the user views shown in the case.
18. Write the QBE statements necessary to implement the database and the user views shown in the case.
19. Implement the database, add sample data, and produce user views shown in the case using an SQL or QBE DBMS.
20. Create a data dictionary for the case.
21. Throughout the narrative and user views, the case assumes that the smallest component of a job is a job category, e.g., framing lumber. Indeed, a different entity could be used. Individual inventory items could be the smallest level with several inventory items comprising a job category. For example, the category of framing lumber could be comprised of pine studs, as well as other lengths of 2x4s, 2x8s, 2x12s, etc. What would be the impact if Bedrock Builders choses to recognize inventory items rather than job categories as the smallest component of a job? What changes in the user views would be needed? Design those user views and draw unnormalized relations from them. Normalize to at least the third normal form. Integrate the relations. Redraw data flow and entity relationship diagrams. Redo SQL or QBE implementation, and the data dictionary.

CHAPTER 8

Eastrim County Supervisors

INTRODUCTION

The voters of Eastrim County, per state law and county ordinances, elect several officials to operate and run the day-to-day business of the county. Those officials include seven County Supervisors, each of whom represents roughly one-seventh of the voters and property in the county. The Board of County Supervisors oversees the administrative affairs of Eastrim County. That includes approving capital construction such as buildings, roads, and bridges. The Board also approves budgets, sets tax and fee rates, and reviews all major changes in county operations. The Board of Supervisors conducts monthly public meetings to discuss important matters, to set policy, and to establish ordinances.

Other elected officials in Eastrim County are the Assessor, the Treasurer, the Clerk, the Sheriff, the County Attorney, and the Clerk of the County Courts.

The County Assessor maintains records of taxable property and appraises the value of that property. A major function of the Assessor's office is to maintain an up-to-date physical survey of Eastrim County. The County Assessor also advises the Board of Supervisors as to the property tax levy schedule that is required to raise sufficient funds to conduct the affairs of the county.

The County Treasurer is responsible for collecting taxes, licenses, and fees due the county. That includes preparing, mailing, and collecting annual property tax notices as well as staffing a customer service counter for collecting motor vehicle taxes and fees for driver and other licenses. The County Treasurer also advises the Board of Supervisors as to the status of the collection of fees and taxes.

The County Clerk is primarily responsible for maintaining official county records. Those include birth, marriage, divorce, and death certificates as well as records of transfer of taxable property, such as bills of sale and wills. The Clerk also maintains archives of records generated by other county offices, such as old property, tax, and census rolls and court records for closed cases. Another important duty is to register voters and conduct elections.

The Sheriff is responsible for enforcing the law and overseeing public safety in Eastrim County. That includes patrolling the county, conducting investigations, coordinating the civil defense network, and operating the Eastrim County Jail.

The County Attorney prosecutes civil and criminal cases in and relating to the county. The office also includes a public defender's function.

The Clerk of the County Court runs the court system in Eastrim County. That includes providing clerical and bailiff assistance to judges, arranging for juries, and collecting fines and payments levied by the court, including child support.

A common scenario exists throughout all of the Eastrim County offices described above. All elected officials need staff and monetary funds to conduct the activities of their offices. That translates to common bookkeeping functions of payroll, personnel, and budgetary accounting. Rather than duplicate each of those accounting functions in each county office, the County Supervisors' Office handles those tasks in a centralized manner.

Another common aspect of all the county offices is the need to maintain facilities, furnishings, and equipment. Rather than expect each office to handle its own maintenance functions, the County Supervisors' Office provides that service. That includes routine janitorial services and building upkeep as well as maintenance and repair of assets, especially county vehicles. The Board of Supervisors is also responsible for maintaining roads and bridges throughout the rural areas of Eastrim County.

The Board of Supervisors hires three professionals to manage the three major functional areas of the County Supervisors' Office. Verjean Seacrest holds the position of Eastrim County Personnel Director. She has the responsibility for orienting new employees and processing all paperwork relevant to personnel issues. She serves as the county's Ombudsperson and Affirmative Action Officer.

The elected officials are each responsible for hiring, supervising, and terminating the employees of their respective offices. Toward that end, Seacrest advises all the elected officials as to personnel policies. She informs them when it is time to evaluate their employees and maintains records of those evaluations. She also coordinates any grievances through the county's formal grievance process.

Seacrest directly supervises a staff of three clerks. They process and file all personnel records. They also handle all the payroll paperwork including calculating and producing monthly payroll earnings statements for all county employees. They coordinate the distribution and direct deposit of the payroll to employees' bank accounts. Each employee of Eastrim County is required to have a personal bank account for the direct deposit. The county has negotiated free accounts with a local bank for any employees who do not otherwise make use of a bank account.

The second professional who works directly for the Board of Supervisors is Al Belton. He is Eastrim County's Budget Director. He and his staff of six clerks pull together all the annual budget requests from the elected officials for approval by the Board of Supervisors. Belton integrates the requests of other agencies for whom the county assesses and collects taxes. Those include school, utility, and conservation districts within the county, plus municipalities, public health care facilities, libraries, and social service offices.

Belton assists the elected officials in preparing their budget requests. He works with the County Assessor and County Treasurer in preparing revenue estimates. He provides the Board of Supervisors with an analysis of all the budget requests and revenue projections.

After budget and revenue plans are approved and go into effect, Belton is responsible for implementing and overseeing the budget. As revenue is collected by the Treasurer, Belton and his staff distribute funds to external agencies and notify all elected officials of their allocations. Belton's office receives purchase requisitions from elected officials and places purchase orders with vendors.

When a vendor delivers an order or performs a service and expects payment from the county, certain conditions must be met. The county will not pay unless the shipment or service is complete. Furthermore, the vendor must attach a copy of Eastrim County's purchase order to the invoice it submits for payment. When those conditions are met, the Eastrim County Budget Office prepares and transmits payments in the form of electronic funds transfers to vendors' bank accounts. It is a prerequisite for doing business with Eastrim County that a vendor be willing to receive payment via electronic funds transfer.

Belton's staff prepares budget reports for review by the elected officials and by the Board of Supervisors. Lastly, the clerks in Belton's office provide clerical and secretarial service to the County Supervisors. That includes greeting visitors, answering the telephone, typing reports and correspondence, and recording the minutes at Board of Supervisors' meetings.

Sheila Banks is the third professional who works directly for the Board of Supervisors. Banks is the Facilities Director for Eastrim County. She is responsible for maintaining the assets owned by the county. That includes supervising building custodians and vehicle mechanics. She contracts for major repairs to facilities and equipment. Banks also has three crews that inspect, make minor repairs on, and perform routine preventative maintenance on roads and bridges.

With her office staff of two clerks, Banks records repairs, sets maintenance schedules, and plans for routine replacement of assets as they wear out. Another of her duties is to prepare long-term budget projections for asset maintenance and replacement. Her emphasis is always on attempting to smooth cash flow requirements for capital item purchases and maintenance operations.

The three professionals work well together. For instance, they have recently worked out a plan for the computerization of their three offices. They have agreed it is most logical to install a database system for the Personnel and Budget Offices, but to defer the computerization of the Facilities Office to a later date. Banks feels that she and many of her subordinates are too new on their jobs to effectively map out information requirements for a database installation. On the other hand, Seacrest and Belton are both able to specify their requirements and are eager to get on with it.

Together, the three of them have convinced the Board of Supervisors to include funds for the installation of a database system within the current budget period. There should be some cost saving in the regular operating budgets of the Personnel and Budget Offices as a result of the use of the new database system. All parties have agreed that any such permanent savings will be transferred to the Facilities Office's budget until that office is finally ready to install its portion of the database.

USER VIEWS: BUDGET OFFICE

In preparation for implementing a database system for the Budget Office, Budget Director Al Belton identified seven user views. The first, as shown in Figure 8-1, reflects the starting point for the flow of data during routine operations of the Budget Office. User view 8-1 is the purchase requisition/purchase order form. The elected officials submit a hand-written or typed copy of the form as a purchase requisition. The Budget Office will enter data from the form into the budget system, which will generate a purchase order to be sent to the vendor. The vendor must send back a copy of the purchase order with an invoice in order to receive payment. Seacrest has designed the forms and the data entry screen so that the same layout is used for all. Thus, one user view suffices for all the activities.

When the county pays a vendor, it does so by means of an electronic transfer of funds. That is accomplished by sending a notice to the vendor's bank with a copy to the vendor. That notice is user view 8-2 and is shown in Figure 8-2.

User view 8-3 is a listing of vendors. It shows the purchase orders placed with the vendors and the status of each. Figure 8-3 illustrates that user view.

Figure 8-1

User View 8-1: Purchase Requisition / Purchase Order

```
                EASTRIM COUNTY BUDGET OFFICE
                         Courthouse
                     Eastrim, Nebraska  68999

                       PURCHASE ORDER

                                              P.O. NUMBER:          95-00143
                                              ORDER DATE:           01/11/95
                                    REQUIRED DELIVERY DATE:         02/01/95


    VENDOR:   Eastrim Printers
              12th and Main
              Eastrim, Nebraska  68999


    SHIP TO:  Office of the County Clerk, Courthouse
    _____

    BUDGET                                              UNIT
    CODE        UNITS         ITEM DESCRIPTION          PRICE        EXTENSION

    50-606      200,000       Ballots for 3/15/95 election,  .10     $ 20,000.00
                              Per attached specifications
                                                                    _____

                                   PURCHASE ORDER AMOUNT:           $ 20,000.00
                                                                    ===========
```

EASTRIM COUNTY

Courthouse

Eastrim, Nebraska 68999

March 22, 1995

First National Bank
10th and Main
Eastrim, Nebraska 68999

This is an authorization to transfer funds from Eastrim County's General Fund Account (1 2324 765) in the amount of $20,000.00 to the account of Eastrim Printers (3 3487 876) as payment of purchase order #95-00143.

Thank you for your cooperation in this cost-containment program.

Sincerely,

Al Belton, Budget Director
Eastrim County Budget Office

cc: Eastrim Printers
　　 12th and Main
　　 Eastrim, NE 68999

Figure 8-2
User View 8-2: Electronic Funds Transfer Notice

Figure 8-3
User View 8-3: Vendor Listing

VENDOR SUMMARY LISTING
June 30, 1995

VENDOR NUMBER	VENDOR NAME	OPEN P.O.'s	RETIRED P.O.'s	YTD PURCHASES
8	Eastrim Printers	.00	12,000.00	12,000.00
12	Eastrim Diesel Supply	857.00	.00	857.00
87	Eastrim Computer Rental	120.00	480.00	600.00
109	Eastrim Office Supply	1338.00	8253.79	9591.79
124	Eastrim Machinery	1150.00	.00	1150.00
176	Bob's Everything Mart	.00	52.39	52.39
857	Sandra's Emporium	142.83	142.83	285.66
1004	Clyde's Legal Service	.00	.00	.00
2323	Furniture To Go	8882.00	1118.00	10,000.00
	TOTALS	12,489.83	22,047.01	34,536.84

The Budget Office prepares a budget report for each county office. The budget report is user view 8-4. A portion of the budget report for the Assessors' Office is shown in Figure 8-4. A budget report presents for each budget category the budget amount, a list of the purchase orders placed but not yet paid — which are called encumbrances, and the purchase orders that have been paid this period. This report can be either printed or displayed.

The Budget Office presents a consolidated budget report for the Board of Supervisors. It shows the budget data for each office without the detailed list of purchase orders. That version of the budget report is user view 8-5 and is shown in Figure 8-5. Like the previous user view, this one can be printed or displayed.

User view 8-6 shows the revenue report the Budget Office prepares for the Board of Supervisors using data supplied by the County Treasurer. Figure 8-6 illustrates that user view.

The last user view (8-7) that Belton identified for the Budget Office is the data entry screen necessary to input the data to produce the revenue report that is the

```
                    EASTRIM COUNTY ASSESSORS' OFFICE
                         DETAIL BUDGET LISTING
                          NONPERSONAL SERVICES
                           as of August 30, 1995
```

BUDGET CODE	ACCOUNT/ VENDOR	ENCUMBRANCE	EXPENDITURE	BUDGET	UNENCUMBERED
30-603	Office supplies			6000.00	
	Home Town Supply		50.00		
	Home Town Supply	25.00			
	Eastrim Office	125.00			
	Copies R Us		200.00		
	Subtotal	150.00	250.00		5600.00
30-605	Postage			10,000.00	
	Post Office		3000.00		
	Post Office	1000.00			
	Subtotal	1000.00	3000.00		6000.00
	etc.				
30 TOTALS		2678.12	6356.87	30,000.00	20,965.01

Figure 8-4

User View 8-4: Detail Budget Report

```
                           EASTRIM COUNTY
                      SUMMARIZED BUDGET REPORT
                        NONPERSONAL SERVICES
                         as of August 30, 1995
```

BUDGET CODE	ACCOUNT/ VENDOR	ENCUMBRANCE	EXPENDITURE	BUDGET	UNENCUMBERED
30	Assessor	2678	6357	30000	20,965
40	Treasurer	5500	4200	45000	35,300
50	Clerk	4321	3412	30000	22,267
60	Sheriff	8354	7446	65000	49,200
70	Courts	2546	2454	25000	20,000
	etc.				
GRAND TOTALS		75,800	57,000	400,000	267,200

Figure 8-5

User View 8-5: Summarized Budget Report

Figure 8-6
User View 8-6: Revenue Report

```
                          EASTRIM COUNTY
                          REVENUE REPORT
                        as of August 30, 1995

                           MONTH-TO-DATE         YEAR-TO-DATE
   REVENUE SOURCE       PROJECTED   ACTUAL    PROJECTED   ACTUAL

Residential Property Tax   50,000    45,122    100,000     92,365
Commercial Property Tax   385,000   390,459    700,000    705,198
Agricultural Property Tax 145,000   234,988    300,000    307,000
Vehicle Registrations     157,000   300,003    350,000    487,654
Driver Licenses             6,000     6,247     12,000     11,987
                              etc.
TOTALS                    900,000 1,220,231  2,000,000  1,900,000
```

previous user view. As indicated in Figure 8-7, the reader ought to be able to design that data entry screen.

USER VIEWS: PERSONNEL OFFICE

In preparation for installing a database system for the Personnel Office, Personnel Director Verjean Seacrest identified seven user views. The first of those, user view 8-8, is the data entry screen used to input pay period data for each employee. The operator enters an employee's social security number, and the system displays the employee's name and hourly rate or salary for verification purposes. The operator then enters the regular and overtime hours worked—if the employee is paid at an hourly rate—as well as any extra addition to the employee's gross pay or deduction from the employee's net pay. The system then calculates and displays taxes and net pay. It also updates and displays all totals for the period, quarter, and year. Once all the data has been input, calculated, and displayed, the entire screen can be printed as a notification given to employees for the pay period. The same view can be used as an inquiry screen if the operator so indicates at the specified point. If a query is intended, the most recent pay period data is displayed, along with quarterly and yearly data. This user view is illustrated by Figure 8-8.

All Eastrim County employees are paid by direct deposit to their individual bank accounts. A notice is sent to the bank to accomplish that, and a copy is given to the employee. That notice is user view 8-9 and is shown in Figure 8-9.

At the end of the quarter, the Personnel Office must file a 941-A wage report with the government. At the end of the year, the county must prepare and distribute W-2 statements of earnings. Figure 8-10 and 8-11 indicate that the reader ought to be able to design those two user views (8-10 and 8-11), as they are virtually identical in format to user views 5-5 and 5-6.

When a new employee is hired, the Personnel Office collects and enters data regarding that employee. Some of the data is used in the payroll system and some of the data is for use in an emergency. Other of the data is used to determine if an employee is eligible for advancement or transfer to other positions. Much of the data is confidential and cannot be used for any adverse personnel action. However, the data is required to be reported to one or more government agencies in a variety of formats. The data entry screen is user view 8-12 and can also be used to modify or change data as appropriate. It is shown in Figure 8-12. When the data is reported, it is typically accessed in a format unique to each instance but well within the capabilities of a standard database language like SQL or

Continued on page 83

Figure 8-7

User View 8-7: Data Entry Screen for Revenue Report. (The reader should use the area above to design this user view, as indicated in the narrative.)

80 Part II Team Cases

```
              PAYROLL DATA ENTRY AND QUERY SCREEN
                      (EMPLOYEE PAY NOTICE)
```

MOST RECENT PAY PERIOD ENDING DATE	SOC SEC NUM	EMPLOYEE'S NAME	SALARY OR HOURLY RATE
09-10-95	562-95-9999	Blossom A. Dew	7.50/hour

	REG. HOURS	O.T. HOURS	REG. PAY	O.T PAY	ADDITION TO GROSS	GROSS PAY
THIS PERIOD:	40.00	5.00	300.00	56.25	0.00	356.25
FOR QUARTER:	120.00	15.00	900.00	168.75	12.00	1080.75
CALENDAR YR:	120.00	15.00	900.00	168.75	12.00	1080.75

	FED TAX	STATE TAX	FICA TAX	INS. PLAN	RET. PLAN	U.S. BOND	MISC DED.	NET PAY
PERIOD:	52.15	21.25	22.50	10.00	.00	.00	13.45	236.90
QTR:	156.45	63.75	67.50	30.00	.00	.00	13.45	749.60
YEAR:	156.45	63.75	67.50	30.00	.00	.00	13.45	749.60

Figure 8-8
User View 8-8: Payroll Data Entry and Query Screen

EASTRIM COUNTY
Courthouse
Eastrim, Nebraska 68999

September 10, 1995

First National Bank
10th and Main
Eastrim, Nebraska 68999

This is an authorization to transfer funds from Eastrim County's General Payroll Account (1 5231 727) in the amount of $236.90 to the account of Blossom A. Dew (7 1729 142) as a payroll payment for the week ending September 10, 1995.

Thank you for your cooperation in this cost-containment program.

Sincerely,

Verjean Seacrest, Personnel Director
Eastrim County Personnel Office

cc: Blossom A. Dew
    116 Heartland Way
    Eastrim, NE 68998

Figure 8-9
User View 8-9: Notice of Electronic Transfer of Payroll Funds

Figure 8-10

User View 8-10: 941-A Quarterly Government Tax Report. (The reader should use the area above to design this user view, as indicated in the narrative.)

Figure 8-11
User View 8-11: W-2 Year-End Wage and Tax Statement. (The reader should use the area above to design this user view, as indicated in the narrative.)

```
PERSONNEL INFORMATION DATA ENTRY DISPLAY

              FIRST NAME:  Blossom
             MIDDLE NAME:  Abigail
               LAST NAME:  Dew
            MAIDEN NAME:  Wilted
                   ALIAS:  Rosie
   CURRENT STREET ADDRESS:  116 Heartland Way
                    CITY:  Eastrim
                   STATE:  NE
                     ZIP:  68998
               TELEPHONE:  308 555-9999
  PREVIOUS STREET ADDRESS:  8247 Heartless Road
                    CITY:  Walsenburro
                   STATE:  CO
                     ZIP:  80009
               TELEPHONE:  719 555-9999
           DATE EMPLOYED:  11-01-94
         DATE TERMINATED:
           DATE OF BIRTH:  06-15-74
   SOCIAL SECURITY NUMBER:  562-95-9999
         BANK FEDERAL ID #:  1243 7653
         BANK ACCOUNT #:  7 1729 142
     NUMBER OF DEPENDENTS:  1
                  GENDER:  female
             ETHNIC/RACE:  Caucasian
                RELIGION:  none given
        RESIDENCY STATUS:  U.S. citizen
      EMERGENCY CONTACT #1:  Dawn Dew
               TELEPHONE:  719 555-9999
      EMERGENCY CONTACT #2:  Donn Dew
               TELEPHONE:  719 555-9999
         PERSONAL DOCTOR:  Jen Geraldsen
                 ADDRESS:  Eastrim Clinic
                    CITY:  Eastrim
                   STATE:  NE
               TELEPHONE:  308 555-1111
             NEXT OF KIN:  Dawn Dew
            RELATIONSHIP:  mother
                 ADDRESS:  Westside Village
                    CITY:  Walsenburro
                   STATE:  CO
                     ZIP:  80009
               TELEPHONE:  719 555-9999
```

Figure 8-12

User View 8-12: Personnel Information Data Entry Display

QBE. Therefore, the user views associated with those queries or reports are not shown herein.

Each nonelected employee of Eastrim County is evaluated each year. The county does not use a standard quantitative personnel evaluation instrument. Rather, each of the elected officials or department heads is required to respond in written sentences to several statements about the employee. That comprises user view 8-13. Figure 8-13 presents that view, which is the format for both the data entry screen and for the query or printed report.

At annual evaluation time, each employee receives a copy of the evaluation and then meets with her/his supervisor to discuss it. Minutes of the meeting are recorded and entered into the personnel system as text, along with information about the meeting itself and a list of the participants. The same technique is used to record any meeting on any personnel action. Figure 8-14 shows that user view 8-14 is used to record and to output such meeting records. The data can later be accessed by date, time, location, topic, meeting participant, or by scanning the text of the minutes for any key words.

After this latter capability has been installed for the Personnel Office, Al Belton intends to evaluate it for use in the Budget Office to record and access the minutes of meetings of the Board of Supervisors. The Clerk of the County Courts thinks it also has potential as a retrieval system for court proceedings.

EMPLOYEE PERFORMANCE EVALUATION
DATA ENTRY AND REPORT FORM

DATE:	November 1, 1995
EMPLOYEE'S NAME:	Blossom A. Dew
SOCIAL SECURITY #:	562-95-9999
JOB TITLE:	Budget Clerk 2
EVALUATOR'S NAME:	Al Belton
SOCIAL SECURITY #:	925-92-5925
JOB TITLE:	Budget Director

1. DESCRIBE HOW WELL THE EMPLOYEE FOLLOWS INSTRUCTIONS AND TO WHAT EXTENT EMPLOYEE REQUIRES SUPERVISION.

Blossom follows directions very well and works with a minimum amount of supervision. This is probably her strongest quality.

2. DESCRIBE THE QUALITY OF THE EMPLOYEE'S WORK.

Most of the time, the quality of Blossom's work is very high. However, there have been a few times when she gets careless with routine mathematics and we have had to redo much of her work. We've discussed this and she appears to be getting better.

3. DISCUSS THE EMPLOYEE'S ABSENTEEISM AND TARDINESS.

Blossom only has missed three days' work in the past year and has called me at home the night before in each case. However, she is much too often tardy getting to work in the morning and after lunch. She needs to show a great deal of improvement.

      etc.

10. DISCUSS HOW WELL THE EMPLOYEE FOLLOWS COUNTY POLICIES.

Blossom follows all county policies except for excessive tardiness as noted in #3, above.

Figure 8-13

User View 8-13: Employee Performance Evaluation Entry and Report

```
                        MEETING MINUTES

      MEETING DATE:    11/15/95
        START TIME:    9:30 AM
          END TIME:    10:15 AM
          LOCATION:    Supervisors' Board Room

      PARTICIPANT #1:  Blossom A. Dew
      PARTICIPANT #2:  Al Belton
      PARTICIPANT #3:  Verjean Seacrest

         etc.

      PARTICIPANT #n:

      MEETING TOPIC:   Formal reprimand for tardiness


      PROCEEDINGS:


      [Note: This field can be a page or more of text.
             Implementation will vary with the DBMS chosen.
             Alternatives may include a variable length text field, unlimited
             size object, or linked text file.]
```

Figure 8-14
User View 8-14: Meeting Minutes Data Entry and Report

STORAGE REQUIREMENTS

In his feasibility study on implementing the database system for the Budget Office, Al Belton performed an analysis of the volumes of data that will be included in the new systems. He calculated that there are normally about 350 vendors from which the county purchases. On the average, 200 purchase orders per month are sent out to the vendors. There is an average of four lines per purchase order.

Verjean Seacrest also performed volume estimates for the Personnel Office's database. The county employs approximately 500 employees, 200 of whom are temporary summer workers. The summer workers are also evaluated each year as part of their exit interview. All together, there are as many as 5000 personnel-related meetings each year for which the Personnel Office will retain minutes. The minutes average a half page per meeting.

The field sizes or attribute widths allocated on the user views contained in Figures 8-1 through 8-14 are a fairly good representation of the storage needs that should be allocated for the database.

EXERCISES

1. Draw a data flow diagram for the Budget Office part of this case.

2. Draw a data flow diagram fo the Personnel Office part of this case.

3. Draw an entity-relationship diagram for the Budget Office part of the case.

4. Draw an entity-relationship diagram for the Personnel Office part of the case.

5. Design appropriate user views for user views 8-7, 8-10, and 8-11.

6. Create a set of unnormalized relations for the Budget Office part of the database in this case.

7. Create a set of unnormalized relations for the Personnel Office part of the database in this case.

8. Normalize the Budget Office relations to at least the third normal form.

9. Normalize the Personnel Office relations to at least the third normal form.

10. Integrate the Budget Office set of normalized relations with the Personnel Office set of normalized relations. Re-normalize the integrated set of relations if needed.

    (Hint: The point at which the two portions integrate is when the data generated by payroll is charged to the various county offices.)

11. Create a data structure diagram for the database in the case following the format in the textbook.

12. Using the volumes given in the case, calculate an estimate of the size of the database.

13. Draw logical access maps (LAMs) and data-base action diagrams (DADs) for each user view presented above.

14. Map the conceptual model of the database in this case to the IMS or other similar hierarchical model.

15. Map the conceptual model of the database in this case to the CODASYL network model.

16. Map the conceptual model of the database in this case to the relational model.

17. Write the SQL statements necessary to implement the database and the user views shown in the case.

18. Write the QBE statements necessary to implement the database and the user views shown in the case.

19. Implement the database, add sample data, and produce user views shown in the case using an available SQL or QBE DBMS.

20. Create a data dictionary for the case.

21. The case narrative indicates that implementing a database for the Facilities Office was deferred to a later date. Assume that the time has now come to accomplish that task. Brainstorm as to the user views required to keep track of asset repair and maintenance history and to establish a long-term schedule for retiring and replacing assets. Design those user views and draw unnormalized relations from them. Then normalize them to at least the third normal form. Integrate the relations. Redraw the data flow and entity-relationship diagrams. Redo the SQL or QBE implementation, and the data dictionary.